# RADIOGRAPHIC ANATOMY & POSITIONING

Mary L. Madigan, RT(R)(M)
Clinical Coordinator
Radiologic Technology Program
Bellevue Community College
Bellevue, Washington

Andrea Gauthier Cornuelle, MS, RT(R)
Associate Professor
Radiologic Technology Program
Department of Allied Health Human
Services & Social Work
Northern Kentucky University
Highland Heights, Kentucky

Diane H. Gronefeld, MEd, RT(R)
Associate Professor
Radiologic Technology Program
Department of Allied Health Human
Services & Social Work
Northern Kentucky University
Highland Heights, Kentucky

APPLETON & LANGE
Stamford, Connecticut

Notice: The authors and the publisher of this volume have taken care to make certain that the doses of drugs and schedules of treatment are correct and compatible with the standards generally accepted at the time of publication. Nevertheless, as new information becomes available, changes in treatment and in the use of drugs become necessary. The reader is advised to carefully consult the instruction and information material included in the package insert of each drug or therapeutic agent before administration. This advice is especially important when using, administering, or recommending new or infrequently used drugs. The authors and publisher disclaim all responsibility for any liability, loss, injury, or damage incurred as a consequence, directly or indirectly, of the use and application of any of the contents of this volume.

Copyright © 1998 by Appleton & Lange
A Simon & Schuster Company

All rights reserved. This book, or any parts thereof, may not be used or reproduced in any manner without written permission. For information, address Appleton & Lange, Four Stamford Plaza, PO Box 120041, Stamford, Connecticut 06912-0041.

97 98 99 00 01 / 10 9 8 7 6 5 4 3 2 1

Prentice Hall International (UK) Limited, *London*
Prentice Hall of Australia Pty. Limited, *Sydney*
Prentice Hall Canada, Inc., *Toronto*
Prentice Hall Hispanoamericana, S.A., *Mexico*
Prentice Hall of India Private Limited, *New Delhi*
Prentice Hall of Japan, Inc., *Tokyo*
Simon & Schuster Asia Pte. Ltd., *Singapore*
Editora Prentice Hall do Brasil Ltda., *Rio de Janeiro*
Prentice Hall, *Upper Saddle River, New Jersey*

ISBN: 0-8385-8237-0

Library of Congress Catalog Card Number:
97-072964

Acquisitions Editor: Kim Davies
Designer: Janice Bielawa

PRINTED IN THE UNITED STATES OF AMERICA

# PREFACE

This pocket manual is designed to augment the text Radiographic Anatomy & Positioning : An Integrated Approach, by Andrea Gauthier Cornuelle and Diane H. Gronefeld (Appleton & Lange, ©1998). The most commonly performed positions/projections from the text are included, and the approach is to simplify these positions/projections as much as is practical for quick and easy reference.

Unique features to this text include:
- Alphabetical ordering of positions for easy access.
- Relevant technical and positioning information.
- Radiograph evaluation criteria that will help facilitate assessment of the radiographs following their completion.
- Breathing instructions on exams that are impacted by respiration.
- An area for notes on each exam, and space to record specific techniques used.

Although patient shielding is not specifically mentioned, it is understood that appropriate gonadal shielding should be used on children and adults of reproductive age.

This pocket book should prove very useful as a resource always available at your fingertips in the clinical site.

Mary L. Madigan

POCKET
MANUAL FOR

# *R*ADIOGRAPHIC
# ANATOMY
# *&*
# POSITIONING

## ► ABDOMEN: AP

### Technical Considerations
- 14″ × 17″ cassette

### Positioning
- Patient supine
- ASISs equidistant from table
- Arms away from body or resting on upper chest

### Central Ray
- Perpendicular to level of iliac crests

### Breathing Instructions
- Expiration

### Radiograph Evaluation Criteria
- Symphysis pubis and lateral margins of abdomen included
- Renal shadows, psoas muscles, transverse processes, lower border of liver visualized
- Symmetrical iliac crests and iliac spines

NOTES

CR

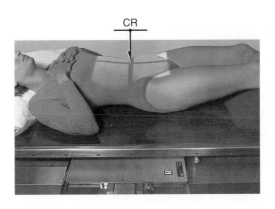

## AP ABDOMEN

| Patient Size | kVp | mAs |
|---|---|---|
| | | |
| | | |
| | | |
| | | |
| | | |
| | | |
| | | |
| | | |
| | | |
| | | |

## ► ABDOMEN: UPRIGHT AP

### Technical Considerations
- 14″ × 17″ cassette

### Positioning
- Patient upright
- ASISs equidistant from Bucky
- Arms at sides

### Central Ray
- Perpendicular to level 2–3″ above iliac crests

### Breathing Instructions
- Expiration

### Radiograph Evaluation Criteria
- Diaphragm and lateral margins of abdomen included
- Renal shadows, psoas muscles visualized
- Symmetrical iliac crests and iliac spines
- Air–fluid levels or free air, if present

---

NOTES

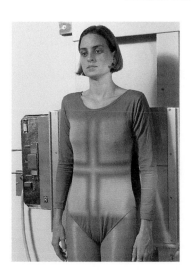

**UPRIGHT AP ADBOMEN**

| Patient Size | kVp | mAs |
| --- | --- | --- |
| | | |
| | | |
| | | |
| | | |
| | | |
| | | |
| | | |
| | | |

## ▶ ABDOMEN: LEFT LATERAL DECUBITUS

### Technical Considerations
- 14″ × 17″ cassette

### Positioning
- Patient on left lateral side
- ASISs equidistant from Bucky
- Arms above level of diaphragm

### Central Ray
- Perpendicular to level 2–3″ above iliac crests

### Breathing Instructions
- Expiration

### Radiograph Evaluation Criteria
- Diaphragm and lateral margins of abdomen included
- Renal shadows, psoas muscles visualized
- Symmetrical iliac crests and iliac spines
- Air–fluid levels or free air, if present

---

NOTES

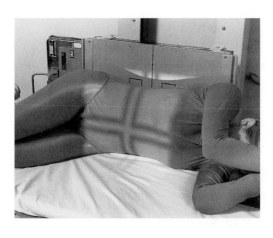

## LEFT LATERAL DECUBITUS ABDOMEN

| Patient Size | kVp | mAs |
|---|---|---|
|  |  |  |
|  |  |  |
|  |  |  |
|  |  |  |
|  |  |  |
|  |  |  |
|  |  |  |
|  |  |  |
|  |  |  |

## ▶ ACROMIOCLAVICULAR JOINTS: AP WITH AND WITHOUT WEIGHTS

### Technical Considerations
- 14″ × 17″ (1/2) or 7″ × 17″ cassette
- Grid
- 72″ SID

### Positioning
- Patient upright
- First exposure without added weights
- Second exposure: hang 5–10 lb weights from patient's wrists

### Central Ray
- Perpendicular to point midway between acromioclavicular joints

### Breathing Instructions
- Expiration to relax shoulders

### Radiograph Evaluation Criteria
- Sternoclavicular joints equidistant from spine
- Bony trabeculae seen
- AC joint not overexposed
- Bilateral joints demonstrated

---

NOTES

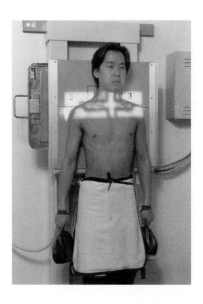

## AP ACROMIOCLAVICULAR JOINTS WITH WEIGHTS

| Patient Size | kVp | mAs |
| --- | --- | --- |
| | | |
| | | |
| | | |
| | | |
| | | |
| | | |
| | | |

# ► AIRWAY: AP UPPER

## Technical Considerations
- 10″ × 12″ cassette
- 40″ SID

## Positioning
- Patient upright
- Patient's chin extended slightly

## Central Ray
- Perpendicular to thyroid cartilage

## Breathing Instructions
- Slow inhalation during exposure

## Radiograph Evaluation Criteria
- C3 to T3 visualized
- Clavicles equidistant from spine
- Mandible superimposed with base of skull
- Air-filled pharynx, larynx, and trachea

NOTES

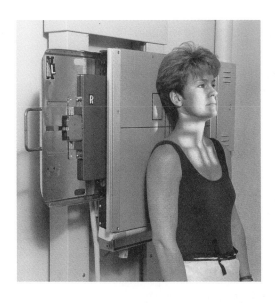

| AP UPPER AIRWAY | | |
|---|---|---|
| Patient Size | kVp | mAs |
| | | |
| | | |
| | | |
| | | |
| | | |
| | | |
| | | |

## ► AIRWAY: LATERAL UPPER

### Technical Considerations
- 10″ × 12″ cassette
- 72″ SID

### Positioning
- Patient upright
- Patient's chin extended slightly
- Arms at sides with shoulders back

### Central Ray
- Perpendicular to point 1–2″ above suprasternal notch

### Breathing Instructions
- Slow inhalation during exposure

### Radiograph Evaluation Criteria
- C1 to T3 visualized
- No rotation of vertebrae
- Mandible slightly elevated
- Air-filled pharynx, larynx, and trachea

---

NOTES

## LATERAL UPPER AIRWAY

| Patient Size | kVp | mAs |
|---|---|---|
| | | |
| | | |
| | | |
| | | |
| | | |
| | | |
| | | |
| | | |

## ▶ ANKLE: AP

### Technical Considerations
- 10″ × 12″ (1/2) cassette
- Detail cassette

### Positioning
- Plantar surface of foot vertical

### Central Ray
- Perpendicular to ankle joint

### Radiograph Evaluation Criteria
- Soft tissue structures included
- Cortex and trabeculae visualized
- Distal fibula and tibia slightly superimposed
- Tibiotalar joint, medial and lateral malleoli, and proximal talus demonstrated

---

NOTES

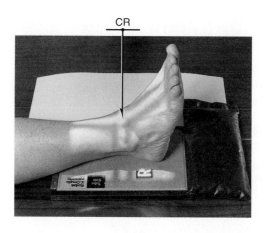

## AP ANKLE

| Patient Size | kVp | mAs |
| --- | --- | --- |
| | | |
| | | |
| | | |
| | | |
| | | |
| | | |
| | | |
| | | |
| | | |

## ▶ ANKLE: MEDIAL OBLIQUE

### Technical Considerations
- 10″ × 12″ (1/2) cassette
- Detail cassette

### Positioning
- Internally rotate leg and foot 15–20°
- Malleoli parallel to plane of film
- Dorsiflex foot

### Central Ray
- Perpendicular to ankle joint

### Radiograph Evaluation Criteria
- Soft tissue structures included
- Cortex and trabeculae visualized
- Mortise joint between proximal talus and distal tibia/fibula demonstrated
- Medial and lateral malleoli, distal tibia/fibula, and proximal talus demonstrated

NOTES

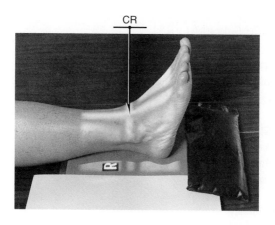

## MEDIAL OBLIQUE ANKLE

| Patient Size | kVp | mAs |
|---|---|---|
| | | |

## ► ANKLE: LATERAL

### Technical Considerations
- 8″ × 10″ cassette
- Detail cassette

### Positioning
- Rotate leg externally
- Patella perpendicular to plane of film
- Dorsiflex foot

### Central Ray
- Perpendicular to ankle joint

### Radiograph Evaluation Criteria
- Soft tissue structures included
- Cortex and trabeculae visualized
- Fibula demonstrated over posterior half of tibia
- Tibiotalar joint demonstrated

NOTES

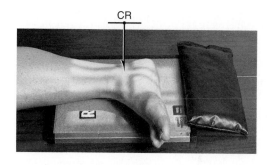

## LATERAL ANKLE

| Patient Size | kVp | mAs |
|---|---|---|
| | | |
| | | |
| | | |
| | | |
| | | |
| | | |
| | | |
| | | |
| | | |
| | | |

C

## ▶ CALCANEUS: AXIAL PLANTODORSAL (OS CALCIS)

### Technical Considerations
- 8″ × 10″ (1/2) or 10″ × 12″ (1/2) cassette
- Detail cassette

### Positioning
- Plantar surface of foot vertical and perpendicular to cassette
- Patient gently pulls back toes with gauze

### Central Ray
- 40° cephalad angle to plantar surface at level of base of 5th metatarsal

### Radiograph Evaluation Criteria
- Soft tissue structures and subtalor joint included
- Cortex and trabeculae visualized
- Calcaneus, sustentaculum tali, tuberosity, trochlear process, and subtalor joint demonstrated

---

NOTES

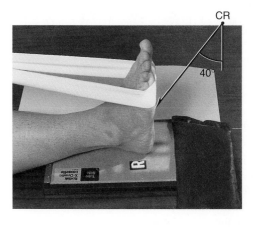

## AXIAL PLANTODORSAL CALCANEUS

| Patient Size | kVp | mAs |
|---|---|---|
| | | |
| | | |
| | | |
| | | |
| | | |
| | | |
| | | |
| | | |
| | | |

C

## ▶ CALCANEUS: LATERAL (OS CALCIS)

### Technical Considerations
- 8″ × 10″ (1/2) or 10″ × 12″ (1/2) cassette
- Detail cassette

### Positioning
- Lateral side of foot down
- Plantar surface of foot perpendicular to cassette

### Central Ray
- Perpendicular to point 1–1½″ distal to medial malleolus

### Radiograph Evaluation Criteria
- Soft tissue structures and 1″ of tibia/fibula included
- Cortex and trabeculae visualized
- Fibula under posterior aspect of tibia
- Calcaneus, tuberosity in profile, and sinus tarsi demonstrated

---

NOTES

C

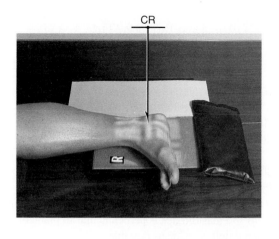

| LATERAL CALCANEUS | | |
|---|---|---|
| Patient Size | kVp | mAs |
| | | |
| | | |
| | | |
| | | |
| | | |
| | | |
| | | |
| | | |
| | | |

C

## ▶ CERVICAL SPINE: AP ATLAS & AXIS (OPEN-MOUTH ODONTOID)

### Technical Considerations
- 8″ × 10″ or 9″ × 9″ cassette
- Grid
- 30–32″ SID

### Positioning
- Patient supine (preferred) or upright
- Raise chin until a line between lower margin of upper teeth and mastoid tips is perpendicular to plane of film
- Open mouth as wide as possible

### Central Ray
- Perpendicular to C1 via open mouth

### Breathing Instructions
- Say "Ah" during exposure

### Radiograph Evaluation Criteria
- Lower edge of upper teeth even with base of skull
- Dens, vertebral body of C2, lateral masses of C1, and zygapophyseal joints between C1 and C2 visualized

---

NOTES

## AP ATLAS AND AXIS CERVICAL SPINE

| Patient Size | kVp | mAs |
|---|---|---|
| | | |
| | | |
| | | |
| | | |
| | | |
| | | |
| | | |

C

## ▶ CERVICAL SPINE: AP

### Technical Considerations
- 10″ × 12″ or 8″ × 10″ cassette
- Grid
- 40″ SID

### Positioning
- Patient supine (preferred) or upright
- Raise chin until a line between upper occlusal plane and mastoid tips is perpendicular to plane of film

### Central Ray
- 15–20° cephalic angle centered to the thyroid cartilage and through C4

### Radiograph Evaluation Criteria
- Soft tissue structures of neck included
- Bony trabeculae visualized
- Intervertebral disc spaces clearly demonstrated
- 3rd–7th vertebral bodies demonstrated

---

NOTES

C

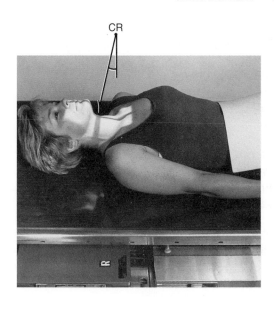

| AP CERVICAL SPINE | | |
|---|---|---|
| Patient Size | kVp | mAs |
| | | |
| | | |
| | | |
| | | |
| | | |
| | | |

C

## ▶ CERVICAL SPINE: AP AXIAL OBLIQUE

### Technical Considerations
- 10″ × 12″ or 8″ × 10″ cassette
- 40″ or 72″ SID
- Grid

### Positioning
- Patient upright (preferred) or supine
- Rotate patient 45°
- Elevate patient's chin slightly
- Both obliques are obtained

### Central Ray
- 15–20° cephalic angle centered to the thyroid cartilage and through C4

### Radiograph Evaluation Criteria
- Soft tissue structures of neck included
- Bony trabeculae visualized
- Intervertebral disc spaces clearly demonstrated
- Mandible away from cervical spine
- Intervertebral foramina and pedicles farthest from the film demonstrated

---

NOTES

C

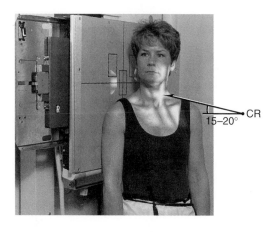

CR
15–20°

## AP AXIAL OBLIQUE CERVICAL SPINE

| Patient Size | kVp | mAs |
|---|---|---|
|  |  |  |
|  |  |  |
|  |  |  |
|  |  |  |
|  |  |  |
|  |  |  |
|  |  |  |
|  |  |  |

C

# ▶ CERVICAL SPINE: LATERAL

## Technical Considerations
- $10'' \times 12''$ or $8'' \times 10''$ cassette
- 72" SID
- Grid

## Positioning
- Patient upright (preferred) or recumbent in true lateral position
- Elevate patient's chin slightly
- Depress shoulders

## Central Ray
- Perpendicular to C4

## Breathing Instructions
- Expiration

## Radiograph Evaluation Criteria
- Soft tissue and bony trabeculae seen
- Mandible away from cervical spine
- Zygapophyseal joints demonstrated
- 1st–7th cervical bodies, intervertebral disc spaces, and spinous processes demonstrated

---

NOTES

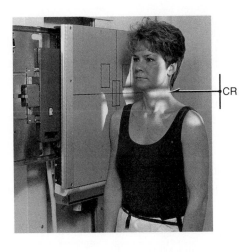

CR

## LATERAL CERVICAL SPINE

| Patient Size | kVp | mAs |
| --- | --- | --- |
|  |  |  |
|  |  |  |
|  |  |  |
|  |  |  |
|  |  |  |
|  |  |  |
|  |  |  |
|  |  |  |
|  |  |  |

C

## ▶ CERVICOTHORACIC SPINE: LATERAL (SWIMMER'S POSITION)

### Technical Considerations
- $10'' \times 12''$ cassette
- Grid

### Positioning
- Patient in true lateral position
- Arm nearest film raised and shoulder anterior; other shoulder depressed and posterior

### Central Ray
- 3–5° caudal angle through T1
- Perpendicular if shoulder depressed

### Breathing Instructions
- Expiration

### Radiograph Evaluation Criteria
- Soft tissue and bony trabeculae seen
- Intervertebral disc spaces and vertebral bodies of C5–T4 demonstrated

---

NOTES

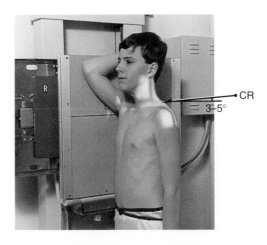

CR

3–5°

| LATERAL CERVICOTHORACIC SPINE | | |
|---|---|---|
| Patient Size | kVp | mAs |
| | | |
| | | |
| | | |
| | | |
| | | |
| | | |
| | | |
| | | |

C

## ▶ CHEST: PA

### Technical Considerations
- 14″ × 17″ cassette
- 72″ SID

### Positioning
- Patient upright
- Top of cassette 1½″ above shoulders
- Back of hands on hips

### Central Ray
- Perpendicular to level of T7

### Breathing Instructions
- 2nd full inspiration

### Radiograph Evaluation Criteria
- Apices, costophrenic angles, and lateral margins of ribs included
- Clavicles equidistant from spine
- Scapulae out of lung field
- 10 posterior ribs demonstrated

---

NOTES

| PA CHEST | | |
|---|---|---|
| Patient Size | kVp | mAs |
| | | |
| | | |
| | | |
| | | |
| | | |
| | | |
| | | |
| | | |

C

# ▶ CHEST: LATERAL

## Technical Considerations
- 14″ × 17″ cassette
- 72″ SID

## Positioning
- Patient upright
- Top of cassette 1½″ above shoulders
- Arms extended over head

## Central Ray
- Perpendicular to level of T7

## Breathing Instructions
- 2nd full inspiration

## Radiograph Evaluation Criteria
- Apices, costophrenic angles, spine, and sternum included
- Heart adequately penetrated
- Patient's arms and/or chin not superimposed over upper lung fields
- Posterior ribs superimposed

---

NOTES

## LATERAL CHEST

| Patient Size | kVp | mAs |
|---|---|---|
| | | |
| | | |
| | | |
| | | |
| | | |
| | | |
| | | |
| | | |

C

## ▶ CHEST: LATERAL DECUBITUS

### Technical Considerations
- 14″ × 17″ cassette
- 72″ SID

### Positioning
- Patient right or left lateral recumbent
- Top of cassette 1½″ above shoulders
- Arms extended over head

### Central Ray
- Perpendicular to level of T7

### Breathing Instructions
- 2nd full inspiration

### Radiograph Evaluation Criteria
- Apices, costophrenic angles, and lateral margins of ribs included
- Lateral margin of lung on side of interest included
- Clavicles equidistant from spine
- Fluid or free air, if present

---

NOTES

C

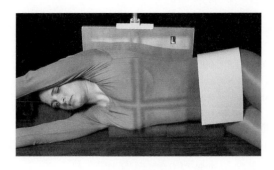

## LATERAL DECUBITUS CHEST

| Patient Size | kVp | mAs |
|---|---|---|
| | | |
| | | |
| | | |
| | | |
| | | |
| | | |
| | | |
| | | |
| | | |
| | | |

C

## ▶ CLAVICLE: AP

### Technical Considerations
- 10″ × 12″ cassette
- Grid

### Positioning
- Shoulders in same transverse plane, parallel to Bucky

### Central Ray
- Perpendicular to midclavicle

### Breathing Instructions
- Inspiration to help elevate and angle the clavicle

### Radiograph Evaluation Criteria
- Sternal and acromial extremities and body of clavicle demonstrated
- Bony trabeculae seen
- Medial half of clavicle superimposed over thorax

---

NOTES

C

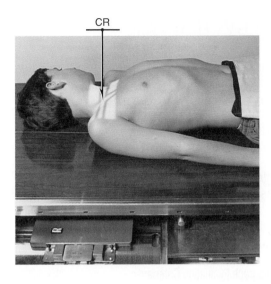

## AP CLAVICLE

| Patient Size | kVp | mAs |
|---|---|---|
| | | |
| | | |
| | | |
| | | |
| | | |
| | | |
| | | |

C

# ▶ CLAVICLE: AP AXIAL

## Technical Considerations
- 10″ × 12″ cassette
- Grid

## Positioning
- Shoulders in same transverse plane, parallel to Bucky

## Central Ray
- 25–30° cephalic angle

## Breathing Instructions
- Inspiration to help elevate and angle the clavicle

## Radiograph Evaluation Criteria
- Sternal and acromial extremities and body of clavicle demonstrated
- Bony trabeculae seen
- Clavicle projected above scapula
- Medial end of clavicle at 1st or 2nd rib

---

NOTES

C

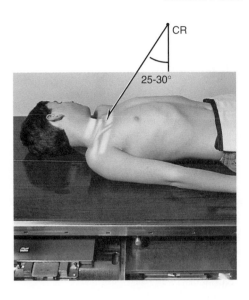

## AP AXIAL CLAVICLE

| Patient Size | kVp | mAs |
|---|---|---|
| | | |
| | | |
| | | |
| | | |
| | | |
| | | |
| | | |

C

# ► COCCYX: AP

## Technical Considerations
- 8″ × 10″ or 9″ × 9″ cassette
- Grid

## Positioning
- Patient supine
- ASISs equidistant from table

## Central Ray
- 10° caudal angle to a point midway between the level of ASIS and symphysis pubis

## Breathing Instructions
- Expiration

## Radiograph Evaluation Criteria
- Coccyx and distal third of sacrum included
- Bony trabeculae seen
- Entire coccyx demonstrated

---

NOTES

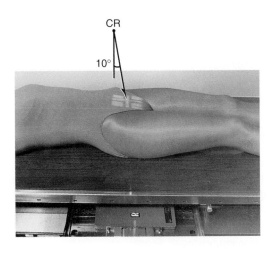

| AP COCCYX | | |
|---|---|---|
| Patient Size | kVp | mAs |
| | | |
| | | |
| | | |
| | | |
| | | |
| | | |
| | | |
| | | |

C

# ▶ COCCYX: LATERAL

## Technical Considerations
- 8″ × 10″ or 9″ × 9″ cassette
- Grid

## Positioning
- Patient in left lateral position

## Central Ray
- Perpendicular to coccyx
- 5″ posterior to midaxillary line

## Breathing Instructions
- Expiration

## Radiograph Evaluation Criteria
- Coccyx and distal third of sacrum included
- Bony trabeculae seen
- Coccyx segments and cornua of coccyx demonstrated

---

NOTES

C

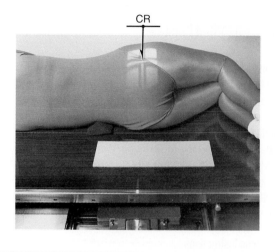

## LATERAL COCCYX

| Patient Size | kVp | mAs |
| --- | --- | --- |
| | | |
| | | |
| | | |
| | | |
| | | |
| | | |
| | | |
| | | |

C

## ▶ COLON: AP/PA

### Technical Considerations
- 14″ × 17″ cassette
- Grid

### Positioning
- Patient supine or prone
- ASISs equidistant from table

### Central Ray
- Perpendicular to level of iliac crests

### Breathing Instructions
- Expiration

### Radiograph Evaluation Criteria
- Entire colon included
- Iliac crests symmetrical
- Cecum; ascending, transverse, and descending colon; and rectum demonstrated

---

NOTES

C

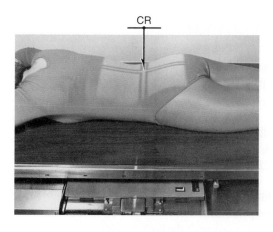

CR

## PA COLON

| Patient Size | kVp | mAs |
|---|---|---|
|  |  |  |
|  |  |  |
|  |  |  |
|  |  |  |
|  |  |  |
|  |  |  |
|  |  |  |
|  |  |  |

C

# ▶ COLON: AP OBLIQUE (RPO & LPO)

## Technical Considerations
- 14″ × 17″ cassette
- Grid

## Positioning
- Rotate into 35–45° posterior oblique position
- RPO and LPO positions

## Central Ray
- Perpendicular to level of iliac crests and 2–3″ lateral to the midline of the body on elevated side

## Breathing Instructions
- Expiration

## Radiograph Evaluation Criteria
- Entire colon included
- RPO–splenic flexure and descending colon demonstrated
- LPO–hepatic flexure, ascending colon, and cecum demonstrated

---

NOTES

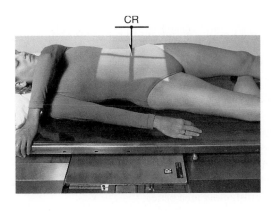

## AP OBLIQUE COLON

| Patient Size | kVp | mAs |
|---|---|---|
| | | |
| | | |
| | | |
| | | |
| | | |
| | | |
| | | |
| | | |

C

# ► COLON: AP/PA AXIAL RECTOSIGMOID

## Technical Considerations
- 11″ × 14″ or 14″ × 17″ cassette
- Grid

## Positioning
- Supine or prone position
- ASISs equidistant from table
- *Or* rotate patient 30–40° LPO/RAO to demonstrate rectosigmoid area better

## Central Ray
- 30–40° cephalic angle to level of ASISs (14″ × 17″)
- 30–40° cephalic angle to a point 2″ inferior to level of ASISs (11″ × 14″) when patient supine
- 30–40° caudad when patient prone

## Breathing Instructions
- Expiration

## Radiograph Evaluation Criteria
- Iliac crests symmetrical
- Rectum and sigmoid colon demonstrated

---

NOTES

C

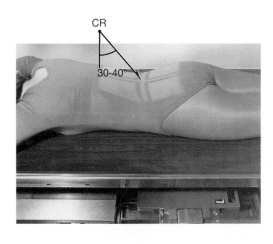

## PA AXIAL RECTOSIGMOID COLON

| Patient Size | kVp | mAs |
|---|---|---|
| | | |
| | | |
| | | |
| | | |
| | | |
| | | |
| | | |
| | | |

C

# ▶ COLON: LATERAL RECTUM

## Technical Considerations
- 10″ × 12″ cassette
- Grid

## Positioning
- Left lateral position
- Patient prone with horizontal beam when performing double contrast study

## Central Ray
- Perpendicular to level of soft tissue depression above greater trochanter of femur

## Breathing Instructions
- Expiration

## Radiograph Evaluation Criteria
- Entire rectosigmoid region included
- Femoral heads superimposed
- Rectum and sigmoid colon demonstrated

---

NOTES

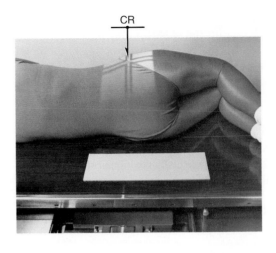

## LATERAL RECTUM

| Patient Size | kVp | mAs |
|---|---|---|
| | | |
| | | |
| | | |
| | | |
| | | |
| | | |
| | | |
| | | |

C

# ▶ COLON: LATERAL DECUBITUS

## Technical Considerations
- 14" × 17" cassette
- Grid

## Positioning
- Patient in right or left lateral position
- Grid cassette vertically positioned so it is centered to iliac crests

## Central Ray
- Horizontal to level of iliac crests

## Breathing Instructions
- Expiration

## Radiograph Evaluation Criteria
- Entire colon included
- Iliac crests symmetrical
- Right lateral—medial side of ascending colon, lateral side of descending colon demonstrated
- Left lateral—lateral side of ascending colon, medial side of descending colon demonstrated

---

NOTES

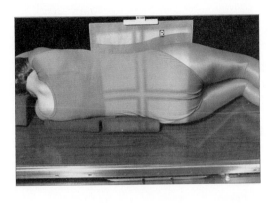

## LATERAL DECUBITUS COLON

| Patient Size | kVp | mAs |
| --- | --- | --- |
| | | |

## ▶ CYSTOGRAM: AP URINARY BLADDER

### Technical Considerations
- 10″ × 12″ cassette
- Grid

### Positioning
- Patient supine
- ASISs equidistant from table

### Central Ray
- 5–20° caudal to point 2″ superior to symphysis pubis

### Breathing Instructions
- Expiration

### Radiograph Evaluation Criteria
- Obturator foramina symmetrical
- Bladder appropriately penetrated
- Urinary bladder, distal ureters (if reflux present), and proximal urethra demonstrated

NOTES

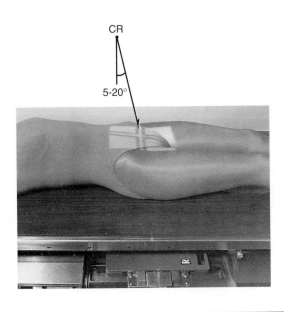

## AP URINARY BLADDER CYSTOGRAM

| Patient Size | kVp | mAs |
|---|---|---|
| | | |
| | | |
| | | |
| | | |
| | | |
| | | |
| | | |

C

## ▶ CYSTOGRAM: AP OBLIQUE URINARY BLADDER

### Technical Considerations
- 10″ × 12″ cassette
- Grid

### Positioning
- Rotate into 40–60° posterior oblique position
- RPO and LPO positions

### Central Ray
- Perpendicular to point 2″ superior to symphysis pubis and 2″ medial to ASIS

### Breathing Instructions
- Expiration

### Radiograph Evaluation Criteria
- Bladder appropriately penetrated
- Elevated thigh not superimposed over bladder
- Urinary bladder, distal ureters (if reflux present), and proximal urethra demonstrated

---

NOTES

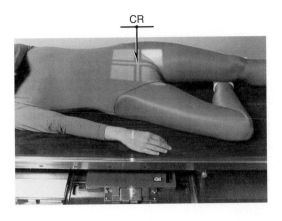

## AP OBLIQUE URINARY BLADDER CYSTOGRAM

| Patient Size | kVp | mAs |
| --- | --- | --- |
| | | |
| | | |
| | | |
| | | |
| | | |
| | | |
| | | |
| | | |
| | | |
| | | |

## ▶ ELBOW: AP

E

### Technical Considerations
- $10'' \times 12''$ (1/2) or $8'' \times 10''$ cassette
- Detail cassette

### Positioning
- Hand supinated
- Humerus in same plane as radius/ulna
- Humeral epicondyles parallel to film

### Central Ray
- Perpendicular to elbow

### Radiograph Evaluation Criteria
- Soft tissue structures, distal third of humerus, and proximal radius/ulna included
- Cortex and trabeculae visualized
- Space between radial head and capitulum visualized
- Medial and lateral epicondyles and condyles, trochlea, capitulum, and radial head and neck demonstrated

---

NOTES

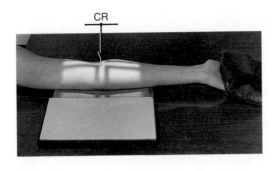

| AP ELBOW | | |
| --- | --- | --- |
| Patient Size | kVp | mAs |
| | | |
| | | |
| | | |
| | | |
| | | |
| | | |
| | | |
| | | |
| | | |
| | | |

E

E

# ▶ ELBOW: MEDIAL (INTERNAL) OBLIQUE

## Technical Considerations
- $10'' \times 12''$ (1/2) or $8'' \times 10''$ cassette
- Detail cassette

## Positioning
- Extend arm and pronate hand until epicondyles form 45° angle with plane of film

## Central Ray
- Perpendicular to elbow joint

## Radiograph Evaluation Criteria
- Soft tissue structures, distal third of humerus and proximal radius/ulna included
- Cortex and trabeculae visualized
- Coronoid process projected free of superimposition and demonstrated in profile

NOTES

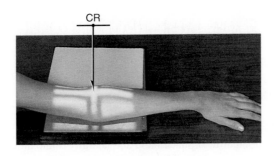

E

## MEDIAL OBLIQUE ELBOW

| Patient Size | kVp | mAs |
| --- | --- | --- |
| | | |
| | | |
| | | |
| | | |
| | | |
| | | |
| | | |
| | | |
| | | |
| | | |
| | | |
| | | |

## ► ELBOW: LATERAL (EXTERNAL) OBLIQUE

### Technical Considerations
- $10'' \times 12''$ (1/2) or $8'' \times 10''$ cassette
- Detail cassette

### Positioning
- Extend arm, supinate hand and laterally rotate until epicondyles form 45° angle with plane of film

### Central Ray
- Perpendicular to elbow joint

### Radiograph Evaluation Criteria
- Soft tissue structures, distal third of humerus and proximal radius/ulna included
- Cortex and trabeculae visualized
- Proximal radioulnar joint demonstrated
- Radius and ulna completely separated
- Ulnar radial notch and radial head, neck, and tuberosity demonstrated

---

NOTES

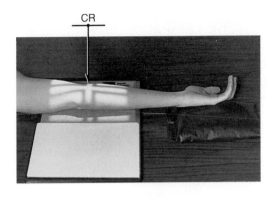

CR

## LATERAL OBLIQUE ELBOW

| Patient Size | kVp | mAs |
| --- | --- | --- |
| | | |
| | | |
| | | |
| | | |
| | | |
| | | |
| | | |
| | | |
| | | |
| | | |

## ► ELBOW: LATERAL

### Technical Considerations
- $10'' \times 12''$ (1/2) or $8'' \times 10''$ cassette
- Detail cassette

### Positioning
- Flex elbow 90°, thumb side of hand up
- Humerus in same plane as radius/ulna
- Epicondyles perpendicular to film

### Central Ray
- Perpendicular to epicondyles

### Radiograph Evaluation Criteria
- Soft tissue structures, distal third of humerus and proximal radius/ulna included
- Cortex and trabeculae visualized
- Radial tuberosity directed anteriorly
- Olecranon process free of superimposition

NOTES

E

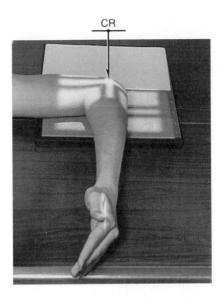

## LATERAL ELBOW

| Patient Size | kVp | mAs |
|---|---|---|
| | | |
| | | |
| | | |
| | | |
| | | |
| | | |

## ▶ ELBOW: AXIAL LATERAL

E

### Technical Considerations
- 8″ × 10″ cassette
- Detail cassette

### Positioning
- Flex elbow 90°, thumb side of hand up
- Humerus in same plane as radius/ulna
- Epicondyles perpendicular to film

### Central Ray
- 45° angle toward shoulder through humeral epicondyles

### Radiograph Evaluation Criteria
- Soft tissue structures, distal humerus, and proximal radius and ulna included
- Cortex and trabeculae visualized
- Elongated image of radial head free of superimposition

NOTES

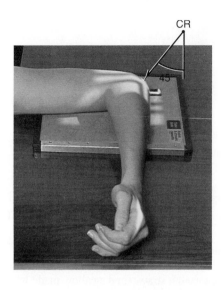

| AXIAL LATERAL ELBOW | | |
|---|---|---|
| Patient Size | kVp | mAs |
|  |  |  |
|  |  |  |
|  |  |  |
|  |  |  |
|  |  |  |
|  |  |  |

## ► ESOPHAGUS: AP

E

### Technical Considerations
• 14″ × 17″ cassette
• Grid

### Positioning
• Patient supine
• Top of cassette 2–3″ above shoulders

### Central Ray
• Perpendicular to midpoint of cassette level of T5–T6

### Breathing Instructions
• Patient takes 1–3 spoonfuls or several drinks of thick barium through straw; final swallow made when instructed
• Exposure made while patient continually swallowing barium

### Radiograph Evaluation Criteria
• Lower part of neck, esophagus, and proximal stomach included
• Barium-filled esophagus from pharynx to cardiac antrum demonstrated

---

NOTES

E

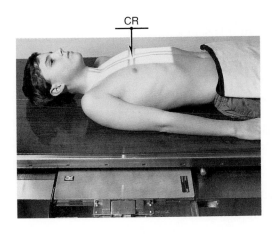

## AP ESOPHAGUS

| Patient Size | kVp | mAs |
|---|---|---|
| | | |
| | | |
| | | |
| | | |
| | | |
| | | |
| | | |
| | | |

E

# ► ESOPHAGUS: RAO

## Technical Considerations
- 14″ × 17″ cassette
- Grid

## Positioning
- Rotate to 35–45° RAO position
- Top of cassette 2–3″ above shoulders

## Central Ray
- Perpendicular to midpoint of cassette level of T5–T6

## Breathing Instructions
- Patient takes 1–3 spoonfuls or several drinks of thick barium through straw; final swallow made when instructed
- Exposure made while patient continually swallowing barium

## Radiograph Evaluation Criteria
- Lower part of neck, esophagus, and proximal stomach included
- Esophagus away from spine
- Barium-filled esophagus from pharynx to cardiac antrum demonstrated

---

NOTES

CR

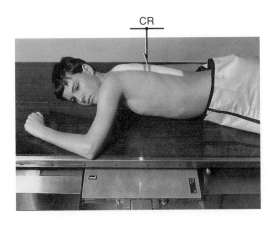

E

## RAO ESOPHAGUS

| Patient Size | kVp | mAs |
|---|---|---|
| | | |
| | | |
| | | |
| | | |
| | | |
| | | |
| | | |
| | | |
| | | |

## ▶ ESOPHAGUS: LATERAL

### Technical Considerations
- 14″ × 17″ cassette
- Grid

### Positioning
- Right or left lateral position
- Top of cassette 2–3″ above shoulders

### Central Ray
- Perpendicular to midpoint of cassette level of T5–T6

### Breathing Instructions
- Patient takes 1–3 spoonfuls or several drinks of thick barium through straw; final swallow made when instructed
- Exposure made while patient continually swallowing barium

### Radiograph Evaluation Criteria
- Lower part of neck, esophagus, and proximal stomach included
- Esophagus away from spine
- Barium-filled esophagus from pharynx to cardiac antrum demonstrated

NOTES

CR

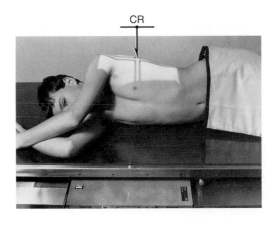

## LATERAL ESOPHAGUS

| Patient Size | kVp | mAs |
|---|---|---|
| | | |

## ▶ EXCRETORY UROGRAM: AP/PA PRE- & POSTCONTRAST URINARY TRACT (IVP: AP/PA)

**E**

### Technical Considerations
- 14″ × 17″ cassette
- Grid

### Positioning
- Patient supine, prone or upright
- ASISs equidistant from table

### Central Ray
- Perpendicular to level of iliac crests

### Breathing Instructions
- Expiration

### Radiograph Evaluation Criteria
- Iliac crests symmetrical
- Preliminary films—renal shadows, psoas muscles, and symphysis pubis demonstrated
- Postinjection—highlighted renal cortex and medullary tissue, major and minor calyces, renal pelves, ureters, and bladder demonstrated

---

NOTES

CR

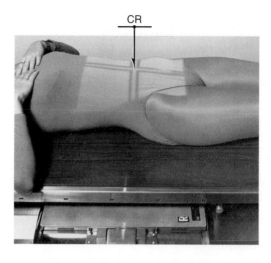

E

## AP ABDOMEN FOR EXCRETORY UROGRAM

| Patient Size | kVp | mAs |
| --- | --- | --- |
| | | |
| | | |
| | | |
| | | |
| | | |
| | | |
| | | |
| | | |

> ## ▶ EXCRETORY UROGRAM: AP COLLIMATED RENAL AREA (IVP: AP RENAL AREA)

**E**

### Technical Considerations
- 11″ × 14″ or 10″ × 12″ cassette
- Grid

### Positioning
- Patient supine
- ASIS equidistant from table

### Central Ray
- Perpendicular to point halfway between xiphoid process and plane of iliac crests

### Breathing Instructions
- Expiration

### Radiograph Evaluation Criteria
- Iliac crests symmetrical
- Preliminary films—renal shadows and psoas muscles demonstrated
- Postinjection—highlighted renal cortex and medullary tissue, major and minor calyces, renal pelves, and proximal ureters demonstrated

---

NOTES

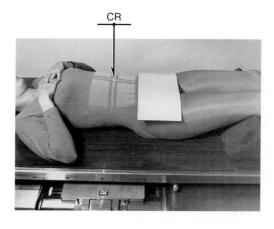

## AP COLLIMATED RENAL AREA EXCRETORY UROGRAM

| Patient Size | kVp | mAs |
|---|---|---|
| | | |
| | | |
| | | |
| | | |
| | | |
| | | |
| | | |
| | | |

## ▶ EXCRETORY UROGRAM: AP OBLIQUE URINARY TRACT (IVP: AP OBLIQUE)

E

### Technical Considerations
- 14″ × 17″ cassette
- Grid

### Positioning
- Rotate into 30° posterior oblique position
- RPO and LPO positions

### Central Ray
- Perpendicular to level of iliac crests

### Breathing Instructions
- Expiration

### Radiograph Evaluation Criteria
- Both kidneys and bladder included
- Kidney nearest film seen in profile
- Up side ureter demonstrated away from spine
- Highlighted renal cortex and medullary tissue, major and minor calyces, renal pelves, ureters, and bladder demonstrated

---

NOTES

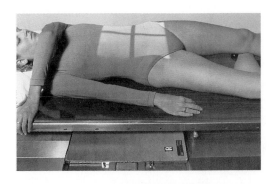

E

## AP OBLIQUE EXCRETORY UROGRAM

| Patient Size | kVp | mAs |
| --- | --- | --- |
| | | |
| | | |
| | | |
| | | |
| | | |
| | | |
| | | |
| | | |
| | | |
| | | |

# ► EXCRETORY UROGRAM: AP URINARY BLADDER (IVP: AP BLADDER)

E

## Technical Considerations
- $10'' \times 12''$ cassette
- Grid

## Positioning
- Patient supine
- ASISs equidistant from table

## Central Ray
- 5–20° caudal to point 2″ superior to symphysis pubis

## Breathing Instructions
- Expiration

## Radiograph Evaluation Criteria
- Obturator foramina symmetrical
- Bladder appropriately penetrated
- Urinary bladder, distal ureters (if reflux present), and proximal urethra demonstrated

NOTES

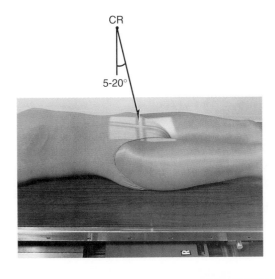

## AP URINARY BLADDER EXCRETORY UROGRAM

| Patient Size | kVp | mAs |
|---|---|---|
|  |  |  |
|  |  |  |
|  |  |  |
|  |  |  |
|  |  |  |
|  |  |  |
|  |  |  |
|  |  |  |

## ▶ FACIAL BONES: PA

### Technical Considerations
- 8″ × 10″ or 9″ × 9″ cassette
- Grid

### Positioning
- Patient's head adjusted until orbitomeatal line perpendicular to plane of film
- Nose and forehead against Bucky

### Central Ray
- 15° caudal for general survey—exit at acanthion
- 25° caudal for orbits—exit at nasion

### Radiograph Evaluation Criteria
- General survey—petrous portions in lower third of orbit, upper ⅔ of orbits, and lower ½ of mandibular rami demonstrated
- Orbits—petrous portions below orbits and orbital margins demonstrated

---

NOTES

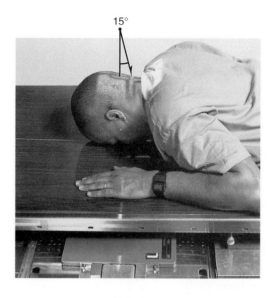

## PA FACIAL BONES

| Patient Size | kVp | mAs |
|---|---|---|
| | | |
| | | |
| | | |
| | | |
| | | |
| | | |

## ► FACIAL BONES: PARIETOACANTHIAL (WATERS)

### Technical Considerations
- 8″ × 10″ cassette
- Grid

### Positioning
- Patient upright or prone
- Orbitomeatal line forms 37° angle to plane of film
- Mentomeatal line perpendicular to plane of film
- Chin resting on Bucky

### Central Ray
- Perpendicular to the casette and exiting at the acanthion

### Radiograph Evaluation Criteria
- Orbits, zygomatic arches, and mandible included
- Petrous ridges projected below maxillary sinuses
- Orbital margins, zygomatic arches, coronoid processes, and bony nasal septum demonstrated

---

NOTES

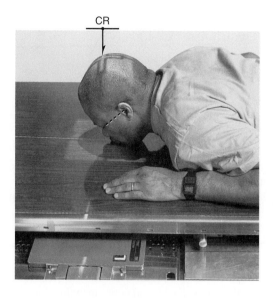

## PARIETOACANTHIAL FACIAL BONES

| Patient Size | kVp | mAs |
|---|---|---|
|  |  |  |
|  |  |  |
|  |  |  |
|  |  |  |
|  |  |  |
|  |  |  |
|  |  |  |

## ► FACIAL BONES: LATERAL

### Technical Considerations
- 8″ × 10″ cassette
- Grid

### Positioning
- Patient upright or recumbent in oblique position, head in true lateral with affected side against Bucky
- Interpupillary line perpendicular to film
- Infraorbital line parallel with transverse axis of film

### Central Ray
- Perpendicular to zygoma

### Radiograph Evaluation Criteria
- Frontal sinuses, EAM, and entire mandible included
- Orbital roofs adequately penetrated
- Orbital roofs superimposed
- Mandibular notches, coronoid processes, rami, bodies, maxilla, and orbits demonstrated

NOTES

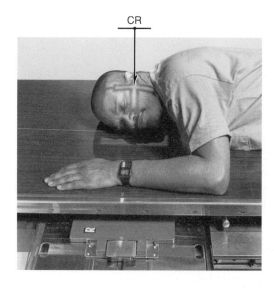

## LATERAL FACIAL BONES

| Patient Size | kVp | mAs |
|---|---|---|
| | | |
| | | |
| | | |
| | | |
| | | |
| | | |
| | | |

## ▶ FEMUR: AP

### Technical Considerations
- 14″ × 17″ or 7″ × 17″ cassette
- Grid

### Positioning
- Middle and distal femur—internally rotate leg 5°
- Proximal femur—internally rotate leg 15°

### Central Ray
- Perpendicular to midpoint of cassette

### Radiograph Evaluation Criteria
- Soft tissue structures and 1–2″ beyond associated joints included
- Cortex and trabeculae visualized
- Femoral head and neck, greater trochanter, femoral shaft, and femoral condyles and epicondyles demonstrated

---

NOTES

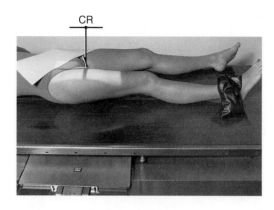

## AP FEMUR, TO INCLUDE HIP

| Patient Size | kVp | mAs |
|---|---|---|
| | | |
| | | |
| | | |
| | | |
| | | |
| | | |
| | | |
| | | |
| | | |
| | | |

## ► FEMUR: LATERAL

### Technical Considerations
- 14″ × 17″ or 7″ × 17″ cassette
- Grid

### Positioning
- Distal femur—femoral condyles perpendicular to plane of film
- Proximal femur—roll pelvis posteriorly to prevent superimposition

### Central Ray
- Perpendicular to midpoint of cassette

### Radiograph Evaluation Criteria
- Soft tissue structures and 1–2″ beyond associated joints included
- Cortex and trabeculae visualized
- Femoral head and neck, lesser trochanter, femoral shaft, and superimposed femoral condyles demonstrated

NOTES

CR

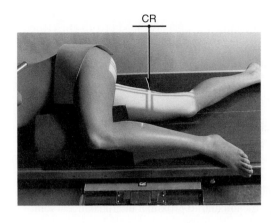

F

## LATERAL FEMUR, TO INCLUDE KNEE

| Patient Size | kVp | mAs |
|---|---|---|
| | | |

## ► FINGERS: PA (2ND–5TH DIGITS)

### Technical Considerations
- 8″ × 10″ (1/3) cassette
- Detail cassette

### Positioning
- Pronate hand
- Separate fingers

### Central Ray
- Perpendicular to proximal interphalangeal joint

### Radiograph Evaluation Criteria
- Soft tissue structures and distal third of metacarpal included
- Cortex and trabeculae visualized
- Proximal, middle, and distal phalanges included
- Interphalangeal joints and metacarpophalangeal joint demonstrated

---

NOTES

F

| PA 4TH DIGIT | | |
|---|---|---|
| Patient Size | kVp | mAs |
| | | |
| | | |
| | | |
| | | |
| | | |
| | | |
| | | |

## ▶ FINGERS: OBLIQUE (2ND–5TH DIGITS)

### Technical Considerations
- 8″ × 10″ (1/3) cassette
- Detail cassette

### Positioning
- Rotate finger 45°
- Finger parallel to cassette

### Central Ray
- Perpendicular to proximal interphalangeal joint

### Radiograph Evaluation Criteria
- Soft tissue structures and distal third of metacarpal included
- Cortex and trabeculae visualized
- Proximal, middle, and distal phalanges included
- Interphalangeal joints and metacarpophalangeal joint demonstrated

---

NOTES

## OBLIQUE 4TH DIGIT

| Patient Size | kVp | mAs |
|---|---|---|
| | | |
| | | |
| | | |
| | | |
| | | |
| | | |
| | | |

## ▶ FINGERS: LATERAL (2ND–5TH DIGITS)

### Technical Considerations
- 8″ × 10″ (1/3) cassette
- Detail cassette

### Positioning
- Rotate finger internally or externally depending on digit
- Finger parallel to cassette

### Central Ray
- Perpendicular to proximal interphalangeal joint

### Radiograph Evaluation Criteria
- Soft tissue structures and distal third of metacarpal included
- Cortex and trabeculae visualized
- Proximal, middle, and distal phalanges included
- Interphalangeal joints demonstrated

---

NOTES

F

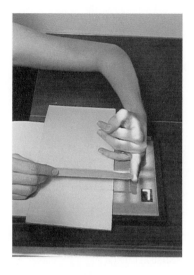

## LATERAL 4TH DIGIT

| Patient Size | kVp | mAs |
|---|---|---|
| | | |
| | | |
| | | |
| | | |
| | | |
| | | |
| | | |

F

## ► FOOT: AP

### Technical Considerations
- $10'' \times 12''$ (1/2) cassette
- Detail cassette

### Positioning
- Plantar surface of foot on cassette

### Central Ray
- 5–15° posterior angle to the base of the third metatarsal
- Angulation varies with height of arch

### Radiograph Evaluation Criteria
- Soft tissue structures included
- Cortex and trabeculae visualized
- Metatarsals, phalanges, proximal, interphalangeal joints, metatarsophalangeal joints, medial and intermediate cuneiforms, and navicular demonstrated

NOTES

CR

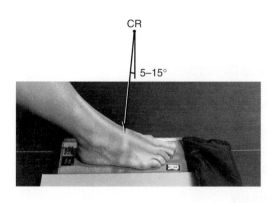

5–15°

F

---

**AP FOOT**

| Patient Size | kVp | mAs |
|---|---|---|
| | | |
| | | |
| | | |
| | | |
| | | |
| | | |
| | | |
| | | |
| | | |

## ► FOOT: MEDIAL OBLIQUE

### Technical Considerations
- $10'' \times 12''$ (1/2) cassette
- Detail cassette

### Positioning
- Internally rotate foot until plantar surface forms 30° angle to cassette

### Central Ray
- Perpendicular to base of third metatarsal

### Radiograph Evaluation Criteria
- Soft tissue structures included
- Cortex and trabeculae visualized
- Bases of 3rd, 4th, and 5th metatarsals nearly free of superimposition
- Phalanges, interphalangeal joints, metatarsophalangeal joints, tarsometatarsal joints, cuboid, lateral cuneiform, sinus tarsi demonstrated

---

NOTES

F

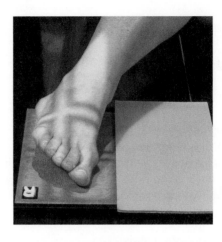

## MEDIAL OBLIQUE FOOT

| Patient Size | kVp | mAs |
|---|---|---|
| | | |
| | | |
| | | |
| | | |
| | | |
| | | |
| | | |
| | | |
| | | |

## ▶ FOOT: LATERAL

### Technical Considerations
- 10″ × 12″ cassette
- Detail cassette

### Positioning
- Lateral side of foot on cassette
- Plantar surface of foot perpendicular to plane of film

### Central Ray
- Perpendicular to tarsometatarsal joints

### Radiograph Evaluation Criteria
- Soft tissue structures and 1″ of tibia/fibula included
- Cortex and trabeculae visualized
- Metatarsals superimposed with base of 5th metatarsal slightly inferior
- Fibula under posterior aspect of tibia
- Calcaneus, talus, and navicular demonstrated

---

NOTES

| LATERAL FOOT | | |
| --- | --- | --- |
| Patient Size | kVp | mAs |
| | | |
| | | |
| | | |
| | | |
| | | |
| | | |
| | | |
| | | |
| | | |
| | | |
| | | |
| | | |

F

## ► FOREARM: AP

### Technical Considerations
- 11" × 14" (1/2) or 10" × 12" (1/2) cassette
- Detail cassette

### Positioning
- Hand supinated
- Humerus in same plane as radius/ulna

### Central Ray
- Perpendicular to middle of forearm

### Radiograph Evaluation Criteria
- Soft tissue structures, carpals, proximal metacarpals, 2" distal humerus included
- Cortex and trabeculae visualized
- Radial tuberosity slightly superimposed over ulna
- Shafts of radius and ulna, radial head and neck, and styloid processes demonstrated

NOTES

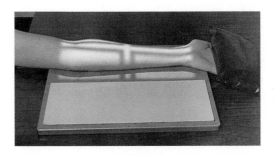

F

## AP FOREARM

| Patient Size | kVp | mAs |
| --- | --- | --- |
| | | |
| | | |
| | | |
| | | |
| | | |
| | | |
| | | |
| | | |
| | | |
| | | |
| | | |

F

# ▶ FOREARM: LATERAL

## Technical Considerations
- 11″ × 14″ (1/2) or 10″ × 12″ (1/2) cassette
- Detail cassette

## Positioning
- Flex elbow 90°, thumb side of hand up
- Humerus in same plane as radius/ulna

## Central Ray
- Perpendicular to middle of forearm

## Radiograph Evaluation Criteria
- Soft tissue structures, carpals, proximal metacarpals, 2″ distal humerus included
- Cortex and trabeculae visualized
- Proximal and distal radius and ulna somewhat superimposed
- Humeral condyles superimposed
- Radial tuberosity directed anteriorly
- Shafts of radius and ulna, olecranon process, and trochlear notch demonstrated

---

NOTES

F

## LATERAL FOREARM

| Patient Size | kVp | mAs |
|---|---|---|
| | | |
| | | |
| | | |
| | | |
| | | |
| | | |
| | | |
| | | |

## ▶ GALLBLADDER: PA (ORAL CHOLECYSTOGRAM)

### Technical Considerations
- 14″ × 17″ or 10″ × 12″ cassette
- Grid

### Positioning
- Patient prone
- Abdominal scout—midsagittal plane to midline of table
- Localized view—sagittal plane between spine and lateral margin of ribs to midline of table

### Central Ray
- Perpendicular to level of iliac crests on scout
- Perpendicular to inferior margin of ribs on localized view

### Breathing Instructions
- Expiration

### Radiograph Evaluation Criteria
- Fundus, body, and neck of gallbladder demonstrated

NOTES

CR

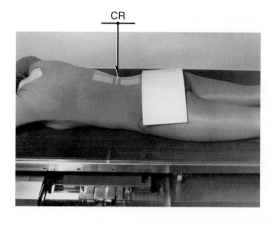

G

## PA GALLBLADDER

| Patient Size | kVp | mAs |
|---|---|---|
| | | |
| | | |
| | | |
| | | |
| | | |
| | | |
| | | |
| | | |
| | | |

## ▶ GALLBLADDER: LAO (ORAL CHOLECYSTOGRAM)

### Technical Considerations
- 10″ × 12″ or 8″ × 10″ cassette
- Grid

### Positioning
- 15–40° LAO position
- Most rotation on asthenic patients
- Sagittal plane between spine and lateral margin of ribs to midline of table

### Central Ray
- Perpendicular to inferior margin of ribs

### Breathing Instructions
- Expiration

### Radiograph Evaluation Criteria
- Fundus, body, and neck of gallbladder demonstrated

---

NOTES

CR

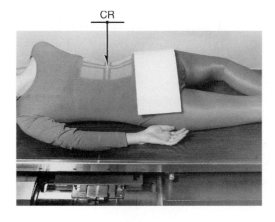

G

## LAO GALLBLADDER

| Patient Size | kVp | mAs |
|---|---|---|
| | | |
| | | |
| | | |
| | | |
| | | |
| | | |
| | | |
| | | |

# ▶ GALLBLADDER: RIGHT LATERAL DECUBITUS (ORAL CHOLECYSTOGRAM)

## Technical Considerations
- 10″ × 12″ or 8″ × 10″ cassette
- Grid

## Positioning
- Patient in right lateral position
- Grid cassette vertically positioned so is centered to inferior margin of ribs

## Central Ray
- Perpendicular to inferior margin of ribs

## Breathing Instructions
- Expiration

## Radiograph Evaluation Criteria
- Fundus, body, neck of gallbladder demonstrated

---

NOTES

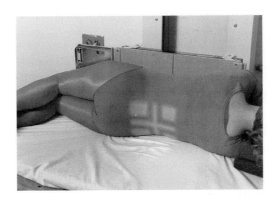

G

## RIGHT LATERAL DECUBITUS GALLBLADDER

| Patient Size | kVp | mAs |
|---|---|---|
| | | |
| | | |
| | | |
| | | |
| | | |
| | | |
| | | |
| | | |
| | | |
| | | |

## ► HAND: PA

### Technical Considerations
- 10″ × 12″ (1/2) or 8″ × 10″ cassette
- Detail cassette

### Positioning
- Hand pronated
- Fingers slightly separated

### Central Ray
- Perpendicular to 3rd metacarpophalangeal joint

### Radiograph Evaluation Criteria
- Soft tissue structures and 1″ distal radius and ulna
- Cortex and trabeculae visualized
- Proximal, middle, and distal phalanges, metacarpals, and carpals included
- Interphalangeal joints, metacarpophalangeal joints, and carpometacarpal joints demonstrated

NOTES

H

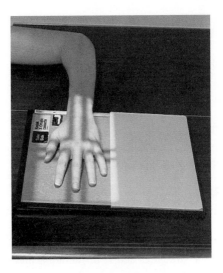

## PA HAND

| Patient Size | kVp | mAs |
| --- | --- | --- |
| | | |
| | | |
| | | |
| | | |
| | | |
| | | |
| | | |
| | | |

## ► HAND: PA OBLIQUE

### Technical Considerations
- $10'' \times 12''$ (1/2) or $8'' \times 10''$ cassette
- Detail cassette

### Positioning
- Rotate hand 45° laterally from pronated position
- Fingers parallel to plane of film

### Central Ray
- Perpendicular to 3rd metacarpophalangeal joint

### Radiograph Evaluation Criteria
- Soft tissue structures and $1''$ distal radius and ulna
- Cortex and trabeculae visualized
- Proximal, middle, and distal phalanges, metacarpals, and carpals demonstrated
- Interphalangeal joints, metacarpophalangeal joints, and carpometacarpal joints demonstrated

---

NOTES

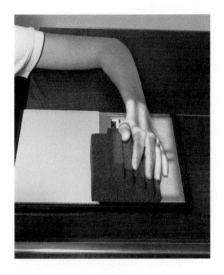

H

## PA OBLIQUE HAND

| Patient Size | kVp | mAs |
|---|---|---|
| | | |
| | | |
| | | |
| | | |
| | | |
| | | |
| | | |

## ► HAND: LATERAL

### Technical Considerations
- 10″ × 12″ (1/2) or 8″ × 10″ cassette
- Detail cassette

### Positioning
- Hand in true lateral with 5th finger resting on cassette
- Extend or fan fingers

### Central Ray
- Perpendicular to metacarpophalangeal joints

### Radiograph Evaluation Criteria
- Soft tissue structures and 1″ distal radius and ulna
- Cortex and trabeculae visualized
- Proximal, middle, distal phalanges included
- 2nd–5th metacarpals superimposed

---

NOTES

H

## LATERAL HAND (FANNED FINGERS)

| Patient Size | kVp | mAs |
|---|---|---|
| | | |
| | | |
| | | |
| | | |
| | | |
| | | |
| | | |

## ► HIP: AP

### Technical Considerations
- 10″ × 12″ cassette
- Grid

### Positioning
- ASISs equidistant from table
- Center cassette to greater trochanter
- Internally rotate leg 15–20° **unless contraindicated**

### Central Ray
- Perpendicular to center of cassette through femoral neck

### Radiograph Evaluation Criteria
- Bony trabeculae visualized
- Greater trochanter in profile; lesser trochanter minimally demonstrated
- Acetabulum, femoral head and neck, greater trochanter, proximal femur, and any prosthetic device included

---

NOTES

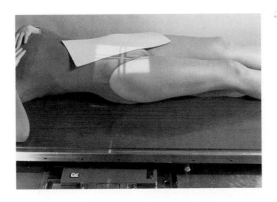

| | AP HIP | |
|---|---|---|
| Patient Size | kVp | mAs |
| | | |
| | | |
| | | |
| | | |
| | | |
| | | |
| | | |
| | | |

## ► HIP: AP OBLIQUE ("FROG-LEG")

### Technical Considerations
- $10'' \times 12''$ cassette
- Grid

### Positioning
- ASISs equidistant from table
- Center cassette to greater trochanter
- Flex hip and knee of affected side
- Abduct affected leg 40°

### Central Ray
- Perpendicular to center of cassette through femoral neck

### Radiograph Evaluation Criteria
- Bony trabeculae visualized
- Greater trochanter superimposed over femoral neck
- Acetabulum, femoral head and neck, proximal femur, and any prosthetic device included

---

NOTES

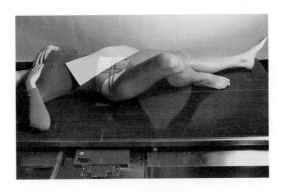

H

## AP OBLIQUE HIP

| Patient Size | kVp | mAs |
|---|---|---|
| | | |
| | | |
| | | |
| | | |
| | | |
| | | |
| | | |
| | | |
| | | |
| | | |
| | | |

## ► HIP: LATERAL (LAUENSTEIN METHOD)

### Technical Considerations
- $10'' \times 12''$ cassette
- Grid

### Positioning
- Rotate toward side of interest
- Flex hip and knee of affected side
- Bring thigh to almost a 90° angle with body and abduct until resting on table
- Center cassette to greater trochanter

### Central Ray
- Perpendicular to center of cassette through femoral neck

### Radiograph Evaluation Criteria
- Bony trabeculae visualized
- Femoral neck seen without foreshortening
- Acetabulum, femoral head and neck, proximal femur, and any prosthetic device included

NOTES

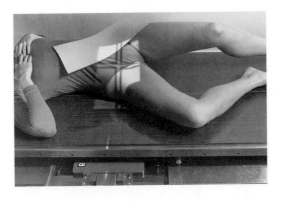

H

## LATERAL HIP (LAUENSTEIN METHOD)

| Patient Size | kVp | mAs |
|---|---|---|
| | | |
| | | |
| | | |
| | | |
| | | |
| | | |
| | | |
| | | |
| | | |
| | | |

## ▶ HIP: TRANSFEMORAL (SURGICAL, CROSS-TABLE) LATERAL

### Technical Considerations
- 10″ × 12″ cassette
- Grid

### Positioning
- Build patient up on pad
- Position grid parallel to neck of femur at the level of the iliac crest
- Internally rotate leg 15–20° **unless contraindicated**
- Elevate unaffected leg

### Central Ray
- Horizontal and at right angles to femoral neck

### Radiograph Evaluation Criteria
- Bony trabeculae visualized
- Femoral neck seen without foreshortening
- Acetabulum, femoral head, proximal femur, and ischial tuberosity included

NOTES

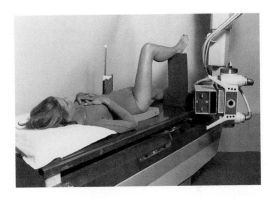

## TRANSFEMORAL LATERAL HIP

| Patient Size | kVp | mAs |
|---|---|---|
| | | |
| | | |
| | | |
| | | |
| | | |
| | | |
| | | |
| | | |
| | | |

H

# ► HUMERUS: AP

## Technical Considerations
- $14'' \times 17''$ or $7'' \times 17''$ cassette
- Grid

## Positioning
- Supinate hand
- Humeral epicondyles parallel to film

## Central Ray
- Perpendicular to midhumerus

## Radiograph Evaluation Criteria
- Soft tissue structures, acromion, glenoid fossa, and $2''$ proximal forearm included
- Cortex and trabeculae visualized
- Greater tubercle in profile
- Humeral head and anatomical and surgical necks demonstrated

---

NOTES

H

## AP HUMERUS

| Patient Size | kVp | mAs |
|---|---|---|
| | | |
| | | |
| | | |
| | | |
| | | |
| | | |
| | | |
| | | |

## ▶ HUMERUS: LATERAL

### Technical Considerations
- 14″ × 17″ or 7″ × 17″ cassette
- Grid

### Positioning
- Internally rotate arm
- Humeral epicondyles perpendicular to film

### Central Ray
- Perpendicular to midhumerus

### Radiograph Evaluation Criteria
- Soft tissue structures, acromion, glenoid fossa, and 2″ proximal forearm included
- Cortex and trabeculae visualized
- Lesser tubercle in profile medially
- Humeral epicondyles superimposed
- Humeral head and surgical neck demonstrated

NOTES

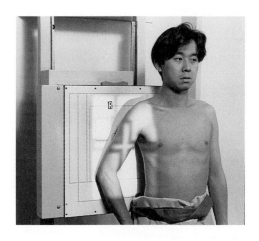

H

## LATERAL HUMERUS

| Patient Size | kVp | mAs |
|---|---|---|
| | | |
| | | |
| | | |
| | | |
| | | |
| | | |
| | | |
| | | |

# ▶ HUMERUS: TRANSTHORACIC LATERAL (NEUTRAL POSITION)

## Technical Considerations
- 10″ × 12″ or 11″ × 14″ cassette
- Grid

## Positioning
- Patient in lateral position
- Affected arm at patient's side toward Bucky and unaffected arm over head

## Central Ray
- Perpendicular to surgical neck

## Breathing Instructions
- Breathing technique
- Full inspiration

## Radiograph Evaluation Criteria
- Head and surgical neck of humerus, acromion process, glenoid fossa, and proximal two thirds of humerus included
- Humerus demonstrated between spine and sternum

---

NOTES

## TRANSTHORACIC LATERAL HUMERUS

| Patient Size | kVp | mAs |
| --- | --- | --- |
| | | |
| | | |
| | | |
| | | |
| | | |
| | | |
| | | |
| | | |

## ▶ KNEE: AP

### Technical Considerations
- 10″ × 12″ or 8″ × 10″ cassette
- Grid or non-grid

### Positioning
- Femoral condyles parallel to plane of film
- Leg may be slightly inverted

### Central Ray
- 5° cephalad to a point ½″ distal to apex of patella

### Radiograph Evaluation Criteria
- Soft tissue structures included
- Cortex and trabeculae visualized
- Proximal fibula and tibia slightly superimposed
- Tibial plateaus, intercondylar eminence, tibial condyle, femoral condyles and epicondyles, and head of fibula demonstrated

NOTES

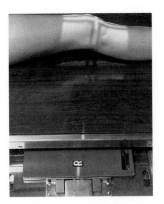

## AP KNEE

| Patient Size | kVp | mAs |
|---|---|---|
| | | |
| | | |
| | | |
| | | |
| | | |
| | | |
| | | |
| | | |
| | | |

## ▶ KNEE: MEDIAL (INTERNAL) OBLIQUE

### Technical Considerations
- 10″ × 12″ or 8″ × 10″ cassette
- Grid or non-grid

### Positioning
- Medially rotate leg until femoral condyles form 45°
  angle to plane of film

### Central Ray
- 5° cephalad to a point ½″ distal to apex of patella

### Radiograph Evaluation Criteria
- Soft tissue structures included
- Cortex and trabeculae visualized
- Half of patella projected medial to femur
- Proximal tibiofibular articulation demonstrated

---

NOTES

CR

5° <

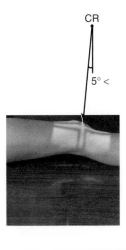

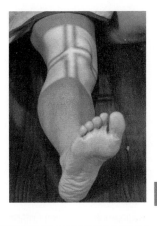

K

## MEDIAL OBLIQUE KNEE

| Patient Size | kVp | mAs |
|---|---|---|
| | | |
| | | |
| | | |
| | | |
| | | |
| | | |
| | | |
| | | |

## ▶ KNEE: LATERAL (EXTERNAL) OBLIQUE

### Technical Considerations
- 10″ × 12″ or 8″ × 10″ cassette
- Grid or non-grid

### Positioning
- Laterally rotate leg until femoral condyles form 45° angle to plane of film

### Central Ray
- 5° cephalad to a point ½″ distal to apex of patella

### Radiograph Evaluation Criteria
- Soft tissue structures included
- Cortex and trabeculae visualized
- Half of patella projected lateral to femur
- Fibula superimposed over proximal tibia

---

NOTES

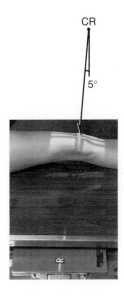

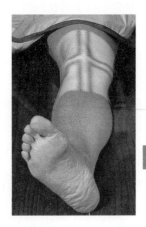

K

## LATERAL OBLIQUE KNEE

| Patient Size | kVp | mAs |
|---|---|---|
| | | |
| | | |
| | | |
| | | |
| | | |
| | | |

## ► KNEE: LATERAL

### Technical Considerations
- $10'' \times 12''$ or $8'' \times 10''$ cassette
- Grid or non-grid

### Positioning
- Flex knee 20–30°
- Femoral condyles perpendicular to plane of film

### Central Ray
- 5° cephalad to a point 1″ inferior to medial femoral condyle

### Radiograph Evaluation Criteria
- Soft tissue structures included
- Cortex and trabeculae visualized
- Patella projected anterior to femur
- Femoral condyles superimposed
- Tibial tuberosity demonstrated

---

NOTES

## LATERAL KNEE

| Patient Size | kVp | mAs |
|---|---|---|
| | | |
| | | |
| | | |
| | | |
| | | |
| | | |
| | | |
| | | |
| | | |
| | | |

K

## ▶ KNEE: PA AXIAL INTERCONDYLAR FOSSA (CAMP–COVENTRY METHOD)

### Technical Considerations
- 8″ × 10″ or 9″ × 9″ cassette
- Grid or non-grid

### Positioning
- With patient prone, flex knee 40–50°
- Rest foot on support

### Central Ray
- Perpendicular to long axis of tibia/fibula through intercondylar fossa
- 40–50° caudal angle

### Radiograph Evaluation Criteria
- Soft tissue structures included
- Cortex and trabeculae visualized
- Medial and lateral femoral condyles symmetrical
- Intercondylar fossa demonstrated

NOTES

## PA AXIAL INTERCONDYLAR FOSSA

| Patient Size | kVp | mAs |
|---|---|---|
|  |  |  |
|  |  |  |
|  |  |  |
|  |  |  |
|  |  |  |
|  |  |  |
|  |  |  |
|  |  |  |
|  |  |  |
|  |  |  |
|  |  |  |
|  |  |  |

## ► LOWER LEG: AP (TIBIA/FIBULA: AP)

### Technical Considerations
- 14″ × 17″ or 7″ × 17″ cassette
- Detail or regular cassette

### Positioning
- Femoral condyles parallel to plane of film
- Dorsiflex foot

### Central Ray
- Perpendicular to midpoint of tibia/fibula

### Radiograph Evaluation Criteria
- Soft tissue structures and 1″ of distal femur and proximal talus included
- Cortex and trabeculae visualized
- Shafts of tibia and fibula, tibial plateau, intercondylar eminence, head of fibula, and medial and lateral malleoli demonstrated

---

NOTES

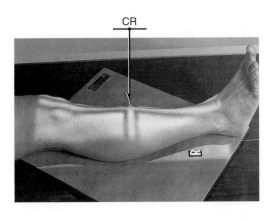

| AP LOWER LEG | | |
|---|---|---|
| Patient Size | kVp | mAs |
| | | |
| | | |
| | | |
| | | |
| | | |
| | | |
| | | |
| | | |

L

## ► LOWER LEG: LATERAL (TIBIA/FIBULA: LATERAL)

### Technical Considerations
- 14″ × 17″ or 7″ × 17″ cassette
- Detail or regular cassette

### Positioning
- Femoral condyles perpendicular to plane of film
- Dorsiflex foot

### Central Ray
- Perpendicular to midpoint of tibia/fibula

### Radiograph Evaluation Criteria
- Soft tissue structures and 1″ of distal femur and proximal talus included
- Cortex and trabeculae visualized
- Medial and lateral femoral condyles superimposed
- Shafts of tibia and fibula and tibial tuberosity demonstrated

---

NOTES

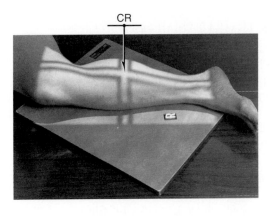

## LATERAL LOWER LEG

| Patient Size | kVp | mAs |
|---|---|---|
| | | |
| | | |
| | | |
| | | |
| | | |
| | | |
| | | |
| | | |
| | | |
| | | |

## ▶ LUMBAR SPINE: AP

### Technical Considerations
- 14″ × 17″ or 11″ × 14″ cassette
- Grid

### Positioning
- Patient supine with knees flexed

### Central Ray
- Perpendicular to L4–L5 (14″ × 17″ film)
- Perpendicular to L3 (11″ × 14″ film)

### Breathing Instructions
- Expiration

### Radiograph Evaluation Criteria
- Iliac crests symmetrical
- Bony trabeculae seen
- Intervertebral disk spaces clearly demonstrated
- Vertebral bodies of L1–L5 and transverse processes demonstrated

NOTES

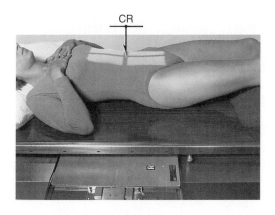

## AP LUMBAR SPINE

| Patient Size | kVp | mAs |
|---|---|---|
| | | |
| | | |
| | | |
| | | |
| | | |
| | | |
| | | |
| | | |
| | | |

## ▶ LUMBAR SPINE: AP OBLIQUE

### Technical Considerations
- 11″ × 14″ cassette
- Grid

### Positioning
- Rotate patient 45°
- Both obliques are obtained

### Central Ray
- Perpendicular to L3 and 2″ medial to ASIS

### Breathing Instructions
- Expiration

### Radiograph Evaluation Criteria
- Bony trabeculae seen
- Zygapophyseal joints nearest the film clearly
  demonstrated
- Articular processes, transverse process, pedicle,
  lamina, and pars interarticularis demonstrated as parts
  of "scotty dog"

---

NOTES

CR

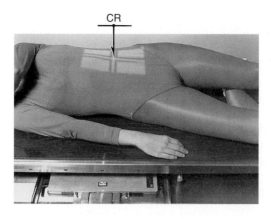

## AP OBLIQUE LUMBAR SPINE

| Patient Size | kVp | mAs |
|---|---|---|
|  |  |  |
|  |  |  |
|  |  |  |
|  |  |  |
|  |  |  |
|  |  |  |
|  |  |  |
|  |  |  |
|  |  |  |
|  |  |  |

L

## ► LUMBAR SPINE: LATERAL

### Technical Considerations
- 14″ × 17″ or 11″ × 14″ cassette
- Grid

### Positioning
- Patient lateral, spine parallel to table

### Central Ray
- Perpendicular to L4–L5 (14″ × 17″ film)
- Perpendicular to L3 (11″ × 14″ film)
- Perpendicular to midaxillary line

### Breathing Instructions
- Expiration

### Radiograph Evaluation Criteria
- Bony trabeculae seen
- Intervertebral disk spaces clearly demonstrated
- Vertebral bodies of L1–L5, pedicles, and intervertebral foramina demonstrated

---

NOTES

## LATERAL LUMBAR SPINE

| Patient Size | kVp | mAs |
|---|---|---|
| | | |
| | | |
| | | |
| | | |
| | | |
| | | |
| | | |
| | | |
| | | |

## ▶ LUMBOSACRAL JUNCTION: AP AXIAL

### Technical Considerations
- 8″ × 10″ or 9″ × 9″ cassette
- Grid

### Positioning
- Patient supine with legs extended

### Central Ray
- 30° (males)–35° (females) cephalic angle to a point
  1½″ inferior to the level of the ASISs.

### Breathing Instructions
- Expiration

### Radiograph Evaluation Criteria
- Bony trabeculae seen
- Iliac crests symmetrical
- L5–S1 intervertebral disk space demonstrated

---

NOTES

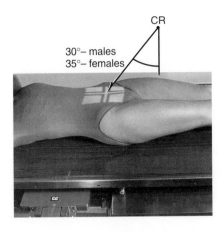

CR

30°– males
35°– females

L

## AP AXIAL LUMBOSACRAL SPINE

| Patient Size | kVp | mAs |
|---|---|---|
| | | |
| | | |
| | | |
| | | |
| | | |
| | | |
| | | |
| | | |
| | | |

# ► LUMBOSACRAL JUNCTION: LATERAL (LUMBAR SPINE: L5–S1 SPOT)

## Technical Considerations
- 8″ × 10″ or 9″ × 9″ cassette
- Grid

## Positioning
- Patient in left lateral position
- Spine parallel to table

## Central Ray
- Parallel to line between iliac crests
- 5° (males)—8° (females) caudal angle
- Should enter body midway between ASIS and crest

## Breathing Instructions
- Expiration

## Radiograph Evaluation Criteria
- Bony trabeculae seen
- L5–S1 intervertebral disk space demonstrated

NOTES

CR

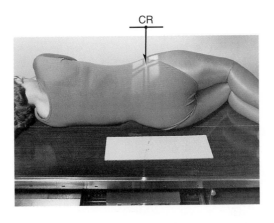

## LATERAL LUMBOSACRAL SPINE

| Patient Size | kVp | mAs |
| --- | --- | --- |
|  |  |  |
|  |  |  |
|  |  |  |
|  |  |  |
|  |  |  |
|  |  |  |
|  |  |  |
|  |  |  |
|  |  |  |
|  |  |  |

L

## ► MANDIBLE: PA

### Technical Considerations
- 8″ × 10″ or 9″ × 9″ cassette
- Grid

### Positioning
- Patient's head adjusted until orbitomeatal perpendicular to plane of film
- Nose and forehead against Bucky

### Central Ray
- Perpendicular to the cassette and exiting at the acanthion

### Radiograph Evaluation Criteria
- Mandibular condyles and rami adequately penetrated
- Petrous ridges symmetrical and filling orbits
- Mandibular rami and lateral portions of mandibular body demonstrated

NOTES

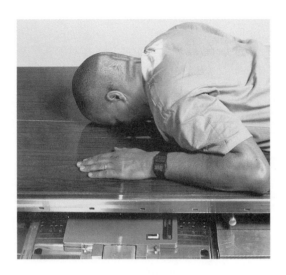

M

## PA MANDIBLE

| Patient Size | kVp | mAs |
|---|---|---|
| | | |
| | | |
| | | |
| | | |
| | | |
| | | |
| | | |
| | | |

## ► MANDIBLE: PA AXIAL MANDIBULAR CONDYLES

### Technical Considerations
- 8″ × 10″ or 9″ × 9″ cassette
- Grid

### Positioning
- Patient's head adjusted until orbitomeatal perpendicular to plane of film
- Nose and forehead against Bucky

### Central Ray
- 20–25° cephalic angle exiting through the acanthion

### Radiograph Evaluation Criteria
- Mandibular condyles and rami adequately penetrated
- Mandibular rami symmetrical
- Petrous ridges fill the orbits
- Mandibular condyles and rami demonstrated

M

---

NOTES

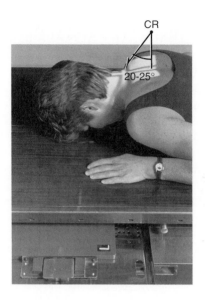

M

## PA AXIAL MANDIBLE

| Patient Size | kVp | mAs |
| --- | --- | --- |
|  |  |  |
|  |  |  |
|  |  |  |
|  |  |  |
|  |  |  |
|  |  |  |
|  |  |  |

## ► MANDIBLE: AXIOLATERAL OBLIQUE

### Technical Considerations
- 8″ × 10″ cassette
- No grid

### Positioning
- Interpupillary line perpendicular to film
- Infraorbitomeatal line parallel with transverse axis of film
- Adjust head so part of greatest interest in parallel to plane of film
  - Ramus—head in true lateral
  - Body—head 30° toward film
  - Mentum—head 45° toward film

### Central Ray
- 15–25° cephalic angle to a point 2″ inferior to gonion away from film

### Radiograph Evaluation Criteria
- Condyle adequately penetrated
- Mandibular ramus, body or mentum demonstrated depending on patient position

---

NOTES

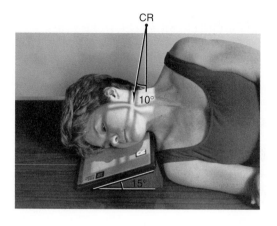

## AXIOLATERAL OBLIQUE MANDIBLE

| Patient Size | kVp | mAs |
|---|---|---|
| | | |
| | | |
| | | |
| | | |
| | | |
| | | |
| | | |
| | | |

M

# ► MANDIBLE: AP AXIAL EXTRAORAL (MANDIBULAR SYMPHYSIS)

## Technical Considerations
- 8″ × 10″ cassette or occlusal film
- Grid

## Positioning
- Patient's chin resting on film holder
- Patient's head adjusted until midsagittal plane perpendicular to plane of film

## Central Ray
- 40–45° toward patient through mandibular symphysis

## Radiograph Evaluation Criteria
- Entire mentum included
- Two halves of mandible symmetrical
- Mandibular symphysis demonstrated

---

NOTES

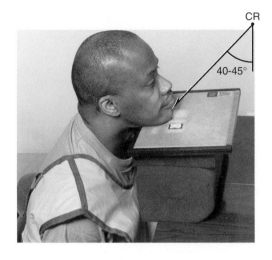

CR

40-45°

M

## AP AXIAL EXTRAORAL MANDIBULAR SYMPHYSIS

| Patient Size | kVp | mAs |
|---|---|---|
| | | |
| | | |
| | | |
| | | |
| | | |
| | | |
| | | |

## ► NASAL BONES: LATERAL

### Technical Considerations
- 8″ × 10″ cassette
- Regular or detail cassette

### Positioning
- Head in lateral position
- Interpupillary line perpendicular to film
- Infraorbital line parallel with the transverse axis of the film

### Central Ray
- Perpendicular to point ¾″ inferior to the nasion

### Radiograph Evaluation Criteria
- Frontonasal junction and anterior nasal spine adequately penetrated
- Nasal bones in profile without rotation
- Nasal bones, soft tissue structures of nose, and anterior nasal spine demonstrated

---

NOTES

CR

| LATERAL NASAL BONES | | |
| --- | --- | --- |
| Patient Size | kVp | mAs |
| | | |
| | | |
| | | |
| | | |
| | | |
| | | |
| | | |
| | | |

# ▶ OPTIC FORAMEN: PARIETO-ORBITAL OBLIQUE (RHESE)

## Technical Considerations
- 8″ × 10″ cassette
- Grid

## Positioning
- Head resting on chin, nose, and cheek of affected side
- Midsagittal plane 53° to plane of film
- Acanthomeatal line parallel with the transverse axis of the film

## Central Ray
- Perpendicular to orbit nearest the film at level of outer canthus

## Radiograph Evaluation Criteria
- Orbit nearest the film adequately penetrated
- Optic canal of side nearest film demonstrated in lower outer quadrant
- Orbital margins and optic canal of dependent side demonstrated
- Both orbits included when imaging orbits for facial bones

NOTES

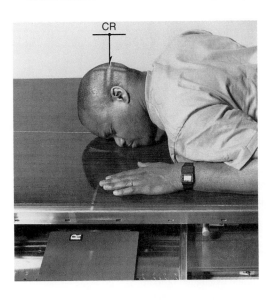

## PARIETO-ORBITAL OBLIQUE OPTIC FORAMEN

| Patient Size | kVp | mAs |
|---|---|---|
| | | |
| | | |
| | | |
| | | |
| | | |
| | | |

## ▶ PARANASAL SINUSES: PA (CALDWELL)

### Technical Considerations
- 8″ × 10″ cassette
- Grid

### Positioning
- Patient upright
- Patient's head adjusted until orbitomeatal line perpendicular to plane of film
- Nose and forehead against Bucky

### Central Ray
- 15° caudal angle to exit at nasion

### Radiograph Evaluation Criteria
- Frontal sinuses, lateral margins of orbits, and maxillary sinuses included
- Orbits adequately penetrated
- Petrous ridges fill lower third of orbits
- Frontal and anterior ethmoid air cells demonstrated

P

---

NOTES

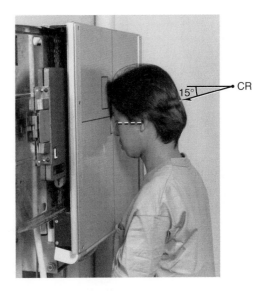

## PA PARANASAL SINUSES

| Patient Size | kVp | mAs |
|---|---|---|
| | | |
| | | |
| | | |
| | | |
| | | |
| | | |
| | | |

# ▶ PARANASAL SINUSES: PARIETOACANTHIAL (WATERS)

## Technical Considerations
- 8″ × 10″ cassette
- Grid

## Positioning
- Patient upright
- Orbitomeatal line forms 37° angle to plane of film
- Mentomeatal line perpendicular to plane of film
- Chin resting on Bucky

## Central Ray
- Perpendicular to film plane and exiting at the acanthion

## Radiograph Evaluation Criteria
- Frontal sinuses, lateral margins of orbits, and maxillary sinuses included
- Orbits adequately penetrated
- Petrous ridges projected below maxillary sinuses
- Maxillary sinuses demonstrated

P

---

NOTES

## PARIETOACANTHIAL PARANASAL SINUSES

| Patient Size | kVp | mAs |
|---|---|---|
| | | |
| | | |
| | | |
| | | |
| | | |
| | | |
| | | |

## ► PARANASAL SINUSES: LATERAL

### Technical Considerations
- 8″ × 10″ cassette
- Grid

### Positioning
- Patient upright with affected side against Bucky in true lateral position
- Interpupillary line perpendicular to film
- Infraorbitomeatal line parallel to floor

### Central Ray
- Perpendicular to point ½–1½″ posterior to outer canthus

### Radiograph Evaluation Criteria
- Frontal, sphenoid, and maxillary sinuses included
- Paranasal sinuses adequately penetrated
- Orbit roofs superimposed
- Frontal, ethmoid, sphenoid, and maxillary sinuses demonstrated

P

---

NOTES

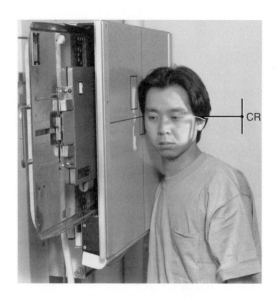

## LATERAL PARANASAL SINUSES

| Patient Size | kVp | mAs |
|---|---|---|
|  |  |  |
|  |  |  |
|  |  |  |
|  |  |  |
|  |  |  |
|  |  |  |
|  |  |  |

P

# ▶ PARANASAL SINUSES: SUBMENTOVERTICAL

## Technical Considerations
- 8″ × 10″ cassette
- Grid

## Positioning
- Head and neck hyperextended
- Infraorbitomeatal line parallel or nearly parallel with plane of film
- Vertex resting on grid device

## Central Ray
- Perpendicular to infraorbitomeatal line to a point 1″ anterior to level of EAMs

## Radiograph Evaluation Criteria
- Nose, mandible, and petrous portion included
- Sphenoid sinuses adequately penetrated
- Petrous portions symmetrical
- Sphenoid and ethmoid sinuses demonstrated

P

---

NOTES

## SUBMENTOVERTICAL PARANASAL SINUSES

| Patient Size | kVp | mAs |
| --- | --- | --- |
| | | |
| | | |
| | | |
| | | |
| | | |
| | | |
| | | |
| | | |
| | | |
| | | |

P

## ► PATELLA: PA

### Technical Considerations
- 8″ × 10″ or 9″ × 9″ cassette
- Grid

### Positioning
- With patient prone, rotate leg so patellar plane is parallel with the plane of film

### Central Ray
- Perpendicular to midpoint of patella

### Radiograph Evaluation Criteria
- Soft tissue structures included
- Cortex and trabeculae visualized
- Proximal fibula and tibia slightly superimposed
- Medial and lateral femoral condyles symmetrical
- Patella to included base and apex demonstrated

P

NOTES

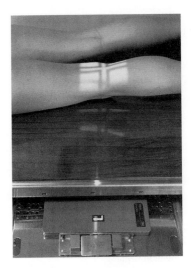

## PA PATELLA

| Patient Size | kVp | mAs |
|---|---|---|
| | | |
| | | |
| | | |
| | | |
| | | |
| | | |
| | | |
| | | |

P

# ▶ PATELLA: LATERAL

## Technical Considerations
- 8″ × 10″ or 9″ × 9″ cassette
- Grid or non-grid

## Positioning
- Rotate patient laterally until femoral condyles perpendicular to film
- Flex knee 5–10°

## Central Ray
- Perpendicular to patellofemoral joint space

## Radiograph Evaluation Criteria
- Soft tissue structures included
- Cortex and trabeculae visualized
- Patella projected anterior to femur
- Femoral condyles superimposed
- Patella and patellofemoral joint space demonstrated

P

NOTES

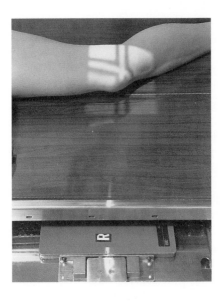

## LATERAL PATELLA

| Patient Size | kVp | mAs |
|---|---|---|
| | | |
| | | |
| | | |
| | | |
| | | |
| | | |
| | | |

P

# ▶ PATELLA: TANGENTIAL

## Technical Considerations
- 8″ × 10″ or 9″ × 9″ cassette
- Non-grid

## Positioning
- With patient prone, slowly flex knee slightly more than 90°

## Central Ray
- 5–10° cephalic angle through patellofemoral joint space and parallel with the plane of the patella

## Radiograph Evaluation Criteria
- Soft tissue structures included
- Cortex and trabeculae visualized
- Patella projected anterior to femur
- Patella, patellofemoral joint space, and femoral condyles demonstrated

P

---

NOTES

CR

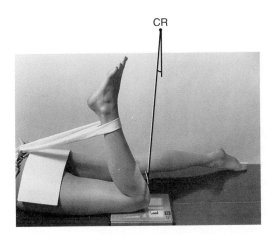

## TANGENTIAL PATELLA

| Patient Size | kVp | mAs |
| --- | --- | --- |
| | | |
| | | |
| | | |
| | | |
| | | |
| | | |
| | | |
| | | |
| | | |

P

## ▶ PELVIS: AP

### Technical Considerations
- 14″ × 17″ cassette
- Grid

### Positioning
- ASISs equidistant from table
- Top edge of cassette 1½–2″ above crest
- Internally rotate legs 15–20° **unless contraindicated**

### Central Ray
- Perpendicular to center of cassette

### Radiograph Evaluation Criteria
- Bony trabeculae visualized
- Obturator foramina and iliac crests symmetrical in size and shape
- Greater trochanters in profile, lesser trochanters minimally demonstrated
- Iliac crests to lesser trochanters included

P

NOTES

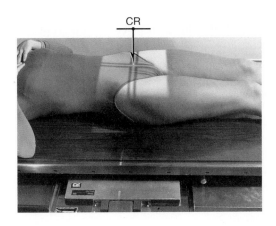

| AP PELVIS | | |
|---|---|---|
| Patient Size | kVp | mAs |
| | | |
| | | |
| | | |
| | | |
| | | |
| | | |
| | | |
| | | |

P

## ▶ PETROUS PORTIONS: MODIFIED LATERAL (LAW)

### Technical Considerations
- 8″ × 10″ cassette
- Grid

### Positioning
- Head rotated from lateral 15° toward face
- Interpupillary line perpendicular to plane of film
- Infraorbitomeatal line parallel with the transverse axis of the film

### Central Ray
- 15° caudal angle to a point 1″ posterior and 2″ superior to EAM on up side

### Radiograph Evaluation Criteria
- Temporal bone adequately penetrated
- Internal and external acoustic meatuses superimposed
- Mastoid air cells and lateral pars petrosa demonstrated

P

---

NOTES

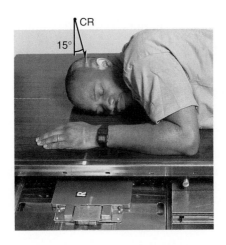

## MODIFIED LATERAL PETROUS PORTIONS

| Patient Size | kVp | mAs |
|---|---|---|
| | | |
| | | |
| | | |
| | | |
| | | |
| | | |
| | | |
| | | |
| | | |

P

# ▶ PETROUS PORTIONS: AXIOLATERAL OBLIQUE (MAYER)

## Technical Considerations
- 8″ × 10″ cassette
- Grid

## Positioning
- Patient supine with head rotated 45° toward side of interest
- Infraorbitomeatal line parallel with the transverse axis of the film

## Central Ray
- 45° caudal angle through EAM nearest the film plane

## Radiograph Evaluation Criteria
- Bony labyrinth adequately penetrated
- Mastoid air cells, EAM, bony labyrinth, and mastoid antrum demonstrated

P

---

NOTES

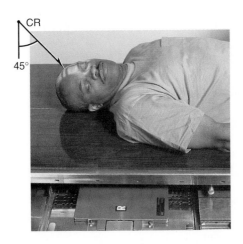

## AXIOLATERAL OBLIQUE PETROUS PORTIONS

| Patient Size | kVp | mAs |
|---|---|---|
| | | |
| | | |
| | | |
| | | |
| | | |
| | | |
| | | |
| | | |

P

## ► PETROUS PORTIONS: POSTERIOR PROFILE (STENVERS)

### Technical Considerations
- 8″ × 10″ cassette
- Grid

### Positioning
- Head resting on forehead, nose, and cheek of affected side
- Midsagittal plane 45° to plane of film
- Infraorbitomeatal line parallel with the transverse axis of the film

### Central Ray
- 12° cephalic angle exiting at the point 1″ anterior to downside EAM

### Radiograph Evaluation Criteria
- Petrous pyramid adequately penetrated
- Internal acoustic canal, mastoid process, mastoid air cells, and petrous ridge demonstrated

---

NOTES

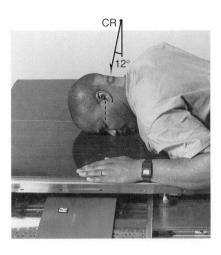

## POSTERIOR PROFILE PETROUS PORTIONS

| Patient Size | kVp | mAs |
|---|---|---|
| | | |
| | | |
| | | |
| | | |
| | | |
| | | |
| | | |
| | | |

P

## ► RIBS AP/PA (ABOVE & BELOW DIAPHRAGM)

### Technical Considerations
- 14″ × 17″ cassette
- Grid

### Positioning
- AP/PA—side of interest closest to film
- Upper ribs—patient upright, top of cassette 2″ above shoulders
- Lower ribs—patient recumbent, bottom of cassette 1″ below iliac crest

### Central Ray
- Perpendicular to midpoint of cassette

### Breathing Instructions
- Upper ribs—inspiration
- Lower ribs—expiration

### Radiograph Evaluation Criteria
- Above the diaphragm—Top 8–10 ribs
- Below the diaphragm—Lower 4–6 ribs

NOTES

CR

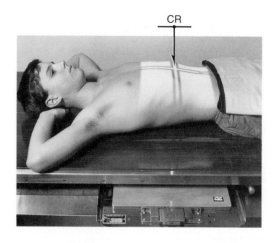

## AP RIBS BELOW DIAPHRAGM

| Patient Size | kVp | mAs |
|---|---|---|
| | | |
| | | |
| | | |
| | | |
| | | |
| | | |
| | | |
| | | |
| | | |

R

## ▶ RIBS AP/PA OBLIQUE

### Technical Considerations
- 14″ × 17″ cassette
- Grid

### Positioning
- Patient upright or recumbent
- Rotate patient 45°, rotate spine away from side of interest
- Right anterior—LAO, left anterior—RAO
- Right posterior—RPO, left posterior—LPO

### Central Ray
- Perpendicular to midpoint of cassette

### Breathing Instructions
- Upper ribs—inspiration
- Lower ribs—expiration

### Radiograph Evaluation Criteria
- Axillary ribs of side nearest the film demonstrated
- Vertebral ribs farthest from the film demonstrated

R

NOTES

## AP OBLIQUE RIBS

| Patient Size | kVp | mAs |
| --- | --- | --- |
| | | |
| | | |
| | | |
| | | |
| | | |
| | | |
| | | |
| | | |
| | | |

R

## ▶ SACROILIAC JOINTS: AP OBLIQUE

### Technical Considerations
- 8″ × 10″ or 10″ × 12″ cassette
- Grid

### Positioning
- Rotate patient's affected side up 25–30º
  - Left SI joint—RPO
  - Right SI joint—LPO
- Both joints examined for comparison

### Central Ray
- Perpendicular to point 1″ medial to ASIS of side farthest from table

### Radiograph Evaluation Criteria
- Bony trabeculae visualized
- Sacroiliac joint, ASIS, and ilium included
- Sacroiliac joint farthest from film demonstrated

NOTES

S

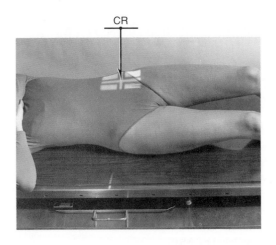

## AP OBLIQUE SACROILIAC JOINTS

| Patient Size | kVp | mAs |
|---|---|---|
| | | |
| | | |
| | | |
| | | |
| | | |
| | | |
| | | |
| | | |
| | | |

S

# ► SACROILIAC JOINTS: AP/PA AXIAL

## Technical Considerations
- 8″ × 10″ or 10″ × 12″ cassette
- Grid

## Positioning
- AP axial—patient supine
- PA axial—patient prone
- Adjust patient's body so there is no rotation

## Central Ray
- AP axial—30–35° cephalic angle entering 1½–2″ below level of ASIS
- PA axial—30–35° caudal angle through lumbosacral joint

## Radiograph Evaluation Criteria
- Bony trabeculae visualized
- Sacroiliac joints, 5th lumbar vertebra, and symphysis pubis included
- Bilateral sacroiliac joints demonstrated

S

NOTES

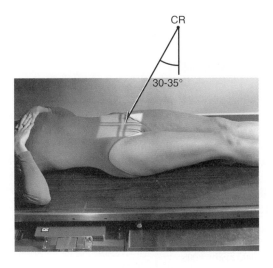

## AP AXIAL SACROILIAC JOINTS

| Patient Size | kVp | mAs |
|---|---|---|
| | | |
| | | |
| | | |
| | | |
| | | |
| | | |
| | | |
| | | |

S

## ► SACRUM: AP

### Technical Considerations
- 10″ × 12″ cassette
- Grid

### Positioning
- Patient supine
- ASISs equidistant from table

### Central Ray
- 15° cephalic angle to a point midway between the level of ASIS and symphysis pubis

### Breathing Instructions
- Expiration

### Radiograph Evaluation Criteria
- Bony trabeculae seen
- Sacral ala symmetrical
- L5–S1 intervertebral disk space, alae, and sacral foramina demonstrated

---

NOTES

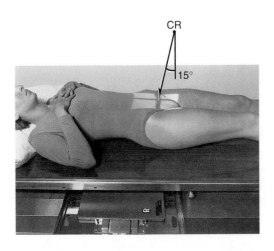

| AP SACRUM | | |
|---|---|---|
| Patient Size | kVp | mAs |
| | | |
| | | |
| | | |
| | | |
| | | |
| | | |
| | | |
| | | |
| | | |

S

## ▶ SACRUM: LATERAL

### Technical Considerations
- 10″ × 12″ cassette
- Grid

### Positioning
- Patient in left lateral position

### Central Ray
- Perpendicular to level of ASIS, 3″ posterior to midaxillary line

### Breathing Instructions
- Expiration

### Radiograph Evaluation Criteria
- Bony trabeculae seen
- Femoral heads nearly superimposed
- Sacral segments, sacral canal, and promontory demonstrated

---

NOTES

S

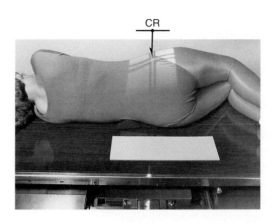

## LATERAL SACRUM

| Patient Size | kVp | mAs |
| --- | --- | --- |
| | | |
| | | |
| | | |
| | | |
| | | |
| | | |
| | | |
| | | |
| | | |

S

## ► SCAPULA: AP

### Technical Considerations
- 10″ × 12″ cassette
- Grid

### Positioning
- Abduct affected arm 90° to body
- Flex affected elbow and supinate hand

### Central Ray
- Perpendicular to midscapula
- 2″ inferior to coracoid process

### Breathing Instructions
- Breathing technique

### Radiograph Evaluation Criteria
- Bony trabeculae seen, lung detail blurred
- Medial scapula under the thorax
- Acromion process, coracoid process, glenoid fossa, and entire body of scapula demonstrated

S    NOTES

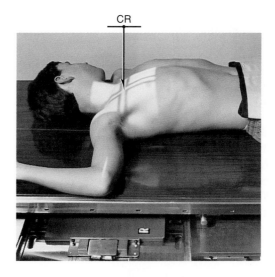

## AP SCAPULA

| Patient Size | kVp | mAs |
| --- | --- | --- |
| | | |
| | | |
| | | |
| | | |
| | | |
| | | |
| | | |
| | | |

S

## ▶ SCAPULA: LATERAL

### Technical Considerations
- 10″ × 12″ cassette
- Grid

### Positioning
- RAO or LAO position
- Rotate patient until affected scapula is perpendicular to Bucky
- Affected arm behind waist for scapular body
- Affected arm above head for acromion and coracoid processes

### Central Ray
- Perpendicular to mid-scapula

### Radiograph Evaluation Criteria
- Bony trabeculae seen
- Acromion process, coracoid process, body of scapula, and inferior angle demonstrated away from thorax

---

NOTES

S

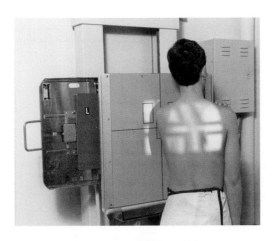

## LATERAL SCAPULA

| Patient Size | kVp | mAs |
|---|---|---|
| | | |
| | | |
| | | |
| | | |
| | | |
| | | |
| | | |
| | | |
| | | |

S

## ▶ SHOULDER: AP EXTERNAL ROTATION

### Technical Considerations
- 10″ × 12″ cassette
- Grid

### Positioning
- Externally rotate arm and supinate hand
- Humeral epicondyles parallel to plane of film

### Central Ray
- Perpendicular to coracoid process

### Radiograph Evaluation Criteria
- Acromion process, surgical neck of humerus, and half of clavicle demonstrated
- Glenohumeral joint adequately penetrated; bony trabeculae seen
- Greater tubercle demonstrated in profile laterally

---

NOTES

S

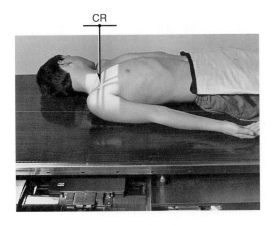

## AP EXTERNAL ROTATION SHOULDER

| Patient Size | kVp | mAs |
|---|---|---|
| | | |
| | | |
| | | |
| | | |
| | | |
| | | |
| | | |
| | | |

S

## ▶ SHOULDER: AP INTERNAL ROTATION

### Technical Considerations
- 10″ × 12″ cassette
- Grid

### Positioning
- Internally rotate arm
- Humeral epicondyles perpendicular to plane of film

### Central Ray
- Perpendicular to coracoid process

### Radiograph Evaluation Criteria
- Acromion process, surgical neck of humerus, and half of clavicle demonstrated
- Glenohumeral joint adequately penetrated; bony trabeculae seen
- Lesser tubercle demonstrated in profile medially
- Greater tubercle superimposed over humeral head

---

NOTES

S

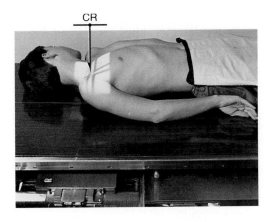

## AP INTERNAL ROTATION SHOULDER

| Patient Size | kVp | mAs |
|---|---|---|
|  |  |  |
|  |  |  |
|  |  |  |
|  |  |  |
|  |  |  |
|  |  |  |
|  |  |  |
|  |  |  |
|  |  |  |
|  |  |  |

S

# ▶ SHOULDER: INFEROSUPERIOR AXIAL (LAWRENCE POSITION)

## Technical Considerations
- $10'' \times 12''$ or $8'' \times 10''$ cassette
- Grid or non-grid

## Positioning
- Affected arm abducted 90°
- Arm in external rotation
- Cassette against superior aspect of shoulder as close to neck as possible

## Central Ray
- 15–30° medial angulation on horizontal beam directed through axilla

## Radiograph Evaluation Criteria
- Glenohumeral joint, acromion process, coracoid process, and humeral surgical neck demonstrated
- Glenohumeral joint adequately penetrated; bony trabeculae seen

S

NOTES

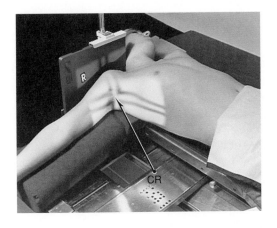

## INFEROSUPERIOR AXIAL SHOULDER

| Patient Size | kVp | mAs |
|---|---|---|
| | | |
| | | |
| | | |
| | | |
| | | |
| | | |
| | | |
| | | |

S

# ▶ SHOULDER: PA OBLIQUE "Y"

## Technical Considerations
- 10″ × 12″ cassette
- Grid

## Positioning
- RAO or LAO position
- Rotate body so midcoronal plane forms 45–60° angle to plane of film
- Dependent scapula perpendicular to Bucky

## Central Ray
- Perpendicular to glenohumeral joint

## Radiograph Evaluation Criteria
- Acromion process, coracoid process, and inferior angle of scapula included
- Glenohumeral relationship demonstrated
- Scapula superimposed over humerus

---

NOTES

S

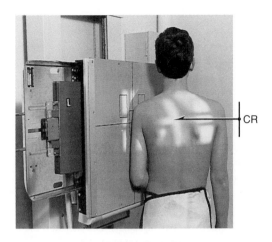

## PA OBLIQUE "Y" SHOULDER

| Patient Size | kVp | mAs |
|---|---|---|
| | | |
| | | |
| | | |
| | | |
| | | |
| | | |
| | | |
| | | |
| | | |

S

## ▶ SKULL: PA (CALDWELL)

### Technical Considerations
- 10″ × 12″ cassette
- Grid

### Positioning
- Patient's head adjusted until orbitomeatal line perpendicular to plane of film
- Nose and forehead against Bucky

### Central Ray
- Perpendicular and exiting at the nasion when the frontal bone is of primary interest
- 15° caudal and exiting at the nasion when a general survey is desired

### Radiograph Evaluation Criteria
- Frontal bone adequately penetrated
- Petrous portions symmetrical
- 0° angle for frontal bone—petrous portions fill orbits
- 15° caudal angle for general survey (Caldwell Method)—petrous portions in lower third of orbit

S

NOTES

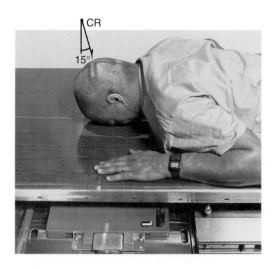

## PA SKULL (CALDWELL)

| Patient Size | kVp | mAs |
|---|---|---|
| | | |
| | | |
| | | |
| | | |
| | | |
| | | |
| | | |
| | | |

S

## ▶ SKULL: AP AXIAL (GRASHEY/TOWNE)

### Technical Considerations
- 10″ × 12″ cassette
- Grid

### Positioning
- Patient supine or upright
- Depress patient's chin until orbitomeatal line is perpendicular to film

### Central Ray
- 30° caudal angle to a point 2½″ above superciliary arches
- 37° caudal angle to infraorbitomeatal line if chin not depressed

### Radiograph Evaluation Criteria
- Occipital bone and foramen magnum adequately penetrated
- Petrous portions symmetrical
- Dorsum sella demonstrated within the foramen magnum
- Occipital bone and lambdoidal suture demonstrated

S

NOTES

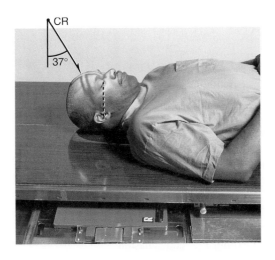

## AP AXIAL SKULL

| Patient Size | kVp | mAs |
|---|---|---|
| | | |
| | | |
| | | |
| | | |
| | | |
| | | |
| | | |

S

# ▶ SKULL: PA AXIAL (HAAS)

## Technical Considerations
- $10'' \times 12''$ cassette
- Grid

## Positioning
- Patient's head adjusted until orbitomeatal line perpendicular to plane of film
- Nose and forehead against Bucky

## Central Ray
- 25–30° cephalic angle entering 1½" inferior to inion and exiting 1½" above nasion

## Radiograph Evaluation Criteria
- Occipital bone and foramen magnum adequately penetrated
- Petrous portions symmetrical
- Dorsum sella demonstrated within the foramen magnum
- Occipital bone and lambdoidal suture demonstrated

S    NOTES

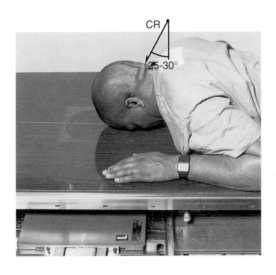

| PA AXIAL SKULL | | |
|---|---|---|
| Patient Size | kVp | mAs |
| | | |
| | | |
| | | |
| | | |
| | | |
| | | |
| | | |
| | | |
| | | |

S

## ▶ SKULL: LATERAL

### Technical Considerations
- 10″ × 12″ cassette
- Grid

### Positioning
- Interpupillary line perpendicular to plane of film
- Infraorbitomeatal line parallel with transverse axis of film

### Central Ray
- Perpendicular to a point 2″ superior to EAM for skull
- Perpendicular to a point ¾″ anterior and ¾″ superior to EAM for sella turcica

### Radiograph Evaluation Criteria
- Vertex, inion, glabella, and C1 included
- Parietal bones adequately penetrated
- Orbital roofs superimposed
- Parietal bones and sella turcica demonstrated

---

NOTES

S

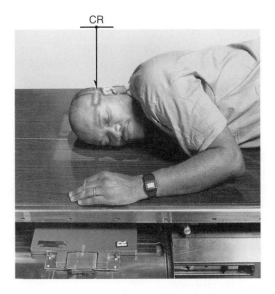

| LATERAL SKULL | | |
|---|---|---|
| Patient Size | kVp | mAs |
| | | |
| | | |
| | | |
| | | |
| | | |
| | | |
| | | |

# ▶ SKULL: SUBMENTOVERTICAL (FULL BASAL)

## Technical Considerations
- 10″ × 12″ cassette
- Grid

## Positioning
- Head and neck hyperextended
- Infraorbitomeatal line parallel or nearly parallel with plane of film
- Vertex resting on grid device

## Central Ray
- Perpendicular to infraorbitomeatal line to a point midway between gonia

## Radiograph Evaluation Criteria
- Nose, mandible, and lateral and posterior margins of skull included
- Basilar structures adequately penetrated
- Petrous portions symmetrical
- Petrous portions, foramen magnum, mandible, and sphenoid sinuses demonstrated

S

NOTES

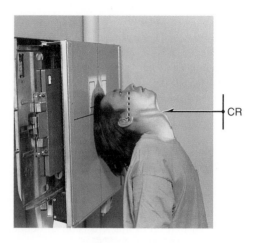

## SUBMENTOVERTICAL SKULL

| Patient Size | kVp | mAs |
|---|---|---|
| | | |
| | | |
| | | |
| | | |
| | | |
| | | |
| | | |
| | | |
| | | |

S

## ▶ SMALL BOWEL: AP/PA

### Technical Considerations
- $14'' \times 17''$ cassette
- Grid

### Positioning
- Patient supine or prone
- ASISs equidistant from table

### Central Ray
- Perpendicular to duodenal bulb (L2) on first exposure
- Perpendicular to level of iliac crests on subsequent exposures

### Breathing Instructions
- Expiration

### Radiograph Evaluation Criteria
- Time marker indicating postingestion time included
- First radiograph—duodenum and jejunum demonstrated
- Subsequent radiographs—jejunum and ileum demonstrated

S

NOTES

CR

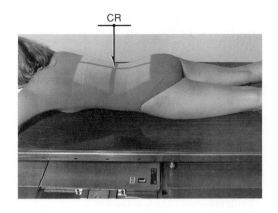

## PA SMALL BOWEL

| Patient Size | kVp | mAs |
| --- | --- | --- |
| | | |
| | | |
| | | |
| | | |
| | | |
| | | |
| | | |
| | | |
| | | |
| | | |

S

# ▶ STERNOCLAVICULAR JOINTS: PA OBLIQUE

## Technical Considerations
- 8″ × 10″ or 9″ × 9″ cassette
- Grid

## Positioning
- Patient in 10–15° RAO & LAO position
- Rotate joint just anterior to vertebrae
- Both joints examined for comparison

## Central Ray
- Perpendicular to suprasternal notch through sternoclavicular joint nearest the film

## Breathing Instructions
- Expiration

## Radiograph Evaluation Criteria
- Sternoclavicular joint nearest the film demonstrated

NOTES

S

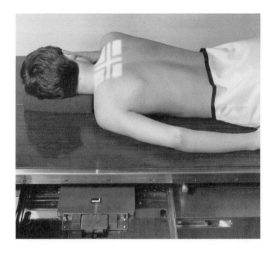

## PA OBLIQUE STERNOCLAVICULAR JOINTS

| Patient Size | kVp | mAs |
|---|---|---|
| | | |
| | | |
| | | |
| | | |
| | | |
| | | |
| | | |
| | | |

S

## ▶ STERNUM: RAO

### Technical Considerations
- 10″ × 12″ cassette
- Grid
- 30″ SID to blur ribs and lung detail

### Positioning
- Patient in 15–20° RAO position
- Patient's right arm at the side and left arm raised

### Central Ray
- Perpendicular to midpoint of sternum at the level of T6–T7

### Breathing Instructions
- Breathing technique

### Radiograph Evaluation Criteria
- Sternum separated from vertebral column and superimposed over cardiac shadow
- Manubrium, body, xiphoid, and sternal angle demonstrated

S

NOTES

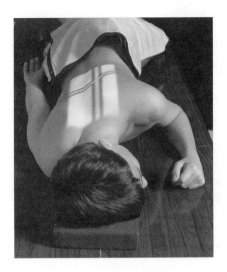

| RAO STERNUM | | |
|---|---|---|
| Patient Size | kVp | mAs |
| | | |
| | | |
| | | |
| | | |
| | | |
| | | |
| | | |
| | | |

S

## ► STERNUM: LATERAL

### Technical Considerations
- $10'' \times 12''$ cassette
- 72″ SID
- Grid

### Positioning
- Upright—rotate shoulders backward
- Supine, horizontal beam—arms up
- Lateral recumbent—arms over head

### Central Ray
- Perpendicular to midpoint of sternum

### Breathing Instructions
- Deep inspiration

### Radiograph Evaluation Criteria
- Sternum separated from ribs and soft tissue of shoulders
- Manubrium, body, xiphoid, and sternal angle demonstrated

S

NOTES

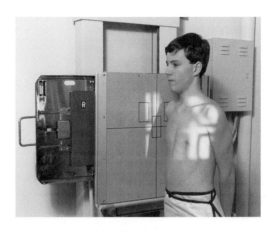

## LATERAL STERNUM

| Patient Size | kVp | mAs |
|---|---|---|
| | | |
| | | |
| | | |
| | | |
| | | |
| | | |
| | | |
| | | |

S

## ► STOMACH: PA (UPPER GI)

### Technical Considerations
- 11″ × 14″ or 14″ × 17″ or 10″ × 12″ cassette
- Grid

### Positioning
- Prone position

### Central Ray
- Perpendicular to level of duodenal bulb
- Sthenic—1–2″ above inferior rib margin
- Hypersthenic—3–4″ above inferior rib margin
- Asthenic—at the inferior rib margin

### Breathing Instructions
- Expiration

### Radiograph Evaluation Criteria
- Entire stomach and duodenum included
- Fundus, barium-filled body, pylorus, duodenal bulb, and C loop demonstrated

---

S   NOTES

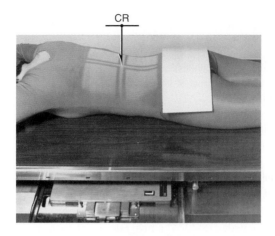

## PA STOMACH

| Patient Size | kVp | mAs |
| --- | --- | --- |
| | | |
| | | |
| | | |
| | | |
| | | |
| | | |
| | | |
| | | |
| | | |

S

## ► STOMACH: AP (UPPER GI)

### Technical Considerations
- 11″ × 14″ or 14″ × 17″ or 10″ × 12″ cassette
- Grid

### Positioning
- Supine position

### Central Ray
- Perpendicular to level of duodenal bulb
- Sthenic—2″ above inferior rib margin
- Hypersthenic—3–4″ above inferior rib margin
- Asthenic—1″ above inferior rib margin

### Breathing Instructions
- Expiration

### Radiograph Evaluation Criteria
- Entire stomach and duodenum included
- Barium-filled fundus, body, pylorus, duodenal bulb, and C loop demonstrated

S    NOTES

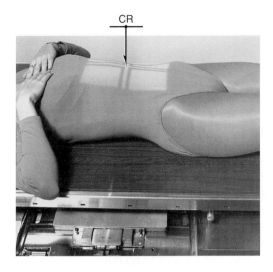

| AP STOMACH | | |
| --- | --- | --- |
| Patient Size | kVp | mAs |
| | | |
| | | |
| | | |
| | | |
| | | |
| | | |
| | | |

S

# ▶ STOMACH: RAO (UPPER GI)

## Technical Considerations
- $11'' \times 14''$ or $10'' \times 12''$ cassette
- Grid

## Positioning
- 40–70° RAO position
- Most rotation on hypersthenic patients

## Central Ray
- Perpendicular to level of duodenal bulb
- Sthenic—1–2″ above inferior rib margin
- Hypersthenic—3–4″ above inferior rib margin
- Asthenic—at the inferior rib margin

## Breathing Instructions
- Expiration

## Radiograph Evaluation Criteria
- Entire stomach and duodenum included
- Fundus, barium-filled body, pyloric canal, duodenal bulb, and C loop demonstrated

**S**

NOTES

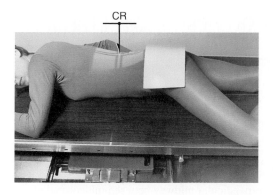

| RAO STOMACH | | |
|---|---|---|
| Patient Size | kVp | mAs |
| | | |
| | | |
| | | |
| | | |
| | | |
| | | |
| | | |
| | | |
| | | |

S

## ▶ STOMACH: LATERAL (UPPER GI)

### Technical Considerations
- 11″ × 14″ or 10″ × 12″ cassette
- Grid

### Positioning
- Patient in right lateral position

### Central Ray
- Perpendicular midway between midcoronal plane and anterior surface of abdomen at level of duodenal bulb
- Sthenic—2″ above inferior rib margin
- Hypersthenic—3–4″ above inferior rib margin
- Asthenic—1″ above inferior rib margin

### Breathing Instructions
- Expiration

### Radiograph Evaluation Criteria
- Entire stomach and duodenum included
- Pyloric canal and duodenal bulb demonstrated

S

NOTES

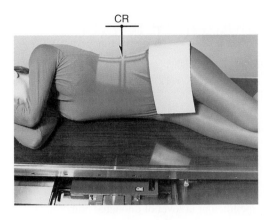

## LATERAL STOMACH

| Patient Size | kVp | mAs |
|---|---|---|
| | | |
| | | |
| | | |
| | | |
| | | |
| | | |
| | | |
| | | |
| | | |
| | | |

S

## ▶ STOMACH: LPO (UPPER GI)

### Technical Considerations
- 11″ × 14″ or 10″ × 12″ cassette
- Grid

### Positioning
- 40–70° LPO position
- Most rotation on hypersthenic patients

### Central Ray
- Perpendicular at level of duodenal bulb
- Sthenic—2″ above inferior rib margin
- Hypersthenic—3–4″ above inferior rib margin
- Asthenic—1″ above inferior rib margin

### Breathing Instructions
- Expiration

### Radiograph Evaluation Criteria
- Entire stomach and duodenum included
- Barium-filled fundus, body, pyloric canal, duodenal bulb, and C loop demonstrated

S

NOTES

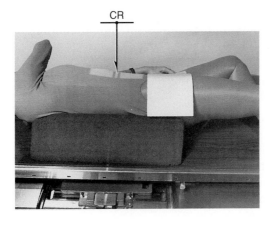

## LPO STOMACH

| Patient Size | kVp | mAs |
|---|---|---|
| | | |

S

# ▶ TEMPOROMANDIBULAR JOINTS: AXIOLATERAL (SHÜLLER)

## Technical Considerations
- 8″ × 10″ cassette
- Grid

## Positioning
- Head lateral
- Interpupillary line perpendicular to film
- Infraorbitomeatal line parallel with transverse axis of film

## Central Ray
- 25–30° caudal angle exiting through TMJ nearest the film

## Radiograph Evaluation Criteria
- Mandibular condyle adequately penetrated
- TMJ farthest from film 2½–3″ below TMJ being examined
- Temporomandibular joint nearest the film demonstrated

---

NOTES

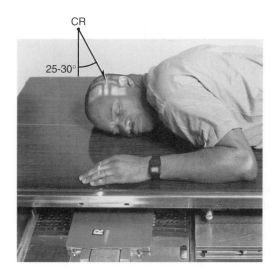

## AXIOLATERAL TEMPOROMANDIBULAR JOINTS

| Patient Size | kVp | mAs |
|---|---|---|
| | | |
| | | |
| | | |
| | | |
| | | |
| | | |
| | | |

T

# ▶ TEMPOROMANDIBULAR JOINTS: AXIOLATERAL OBLIQUE (LAW)

## Technical Considerations
- 8″ × 10″ cassette
- Grid

## Positioning
- Head rotated from lateral 15° toward face
- Acanthomeatal line parallel with the transverse axis of film

## Central Ray
- 15° caudal angle exiting through TMJ nearest the film

## Radiograph Evaluation Criteria
- Mandibular condyle adequately penetrated
- TMJ farthest from film 1½″ anterior and inferior to TMJ being examined
- Temporomandibular joint nearest the film demonstrated

---

NOTES

T

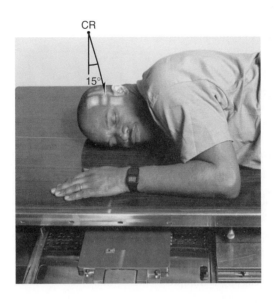

## AXIOLATERAL OBLIQUE TEMPOROMANDIBULAR JOINTS

| Patient Size | kVp | mAs |
|---|---|---|
| | | |
| | | |
| | | |
| | | |
| | | |
| | | |

T

## ▶ THORACIC SPINE: AP

### Technical Considerations
- 14″ × 17″ or 7″ × 17″ cassette
- Grid

### Positioning
- Patient supine with head toward anode
- Top of cassette 1½–2″ over shoulders

### Central Ray
- Perpendicular to a point 3–4″ below suprasternal notch through T7

### Breathing Instructions
- Breathing technique
- Expiration

### Radiograph Evaluation Criteria
- Bony trabeculae seen
- Intervertebral disk spaces clearly demonstrated
- Vertebral bodies of C7–L1 demonstrated

---

NOTES

T

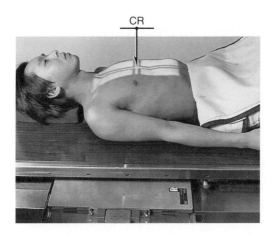

## AP THORACIC SPINE

| Patient Size | kVp | mAs |
|---|---|---|
| | | |
| | | |
| | | |
| | | |
| | | |
| | | |
| | | |
| | | |
| | | |

T

## ▶ THORACIC SPINE: LATERAL

### Technical Considerations
- 14″ × 17″ or 7″ × 17″ cassette
- Grid

### Positioning
- Patient lateral; spine parallel to table
- Arms at right angles to body
- Top of cassette 1½–2″ over shoulders

### Central Ray
- Perpendicular to a point 3–4″ below suprasternal notch through T7
- Perpendicular to midaxillary line

### Breathing Instructions
- Breathing technique

### Radiograph Evaluation Criteria
- Bony trabeculae seen
- Intervertebral foramina superimposed
- Intervertebral disk spaces visualized
- Vertebral bodies of T3–T12 demonstrated

T

NOTES

## LATERAL THORACIC SPINE

| Patient Size | kVp | mAs |
|---|---|---|
| | | |

T

## ▶ THUMB: AP (1ST DIGIT)

### Technical Considerations
- 8″ × 10″ (1/3)
- Detail cassette

### Positioning
- Internally rotate hand until dorsal surface of thumb on cassette

### Central Ray
- Perpendicular to metacarpophalangeal joint

### Radiograph Evaluation Criteria
- Soft tissue structures and trapezium included
- Cortex and trabeculae visualized and sharp
- Proximal and distal phalanges, metacarpal demo
- Interphalangeal joint, metacarpophalangeal joint, and carpometacarpal joint demonstrated

---

NOTES

T

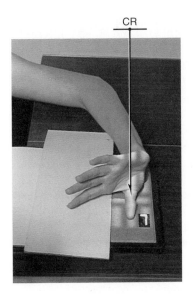

| AP THUMB | | |
|---|---|---|
| Patient Size | kVp | mAs |
| | | |
| | | |
| | | |
| | | |
| | | |
| | | |
| | | |

T

## ► THUMB: OBLIQUE (1ST DIGIT)

### Technical Considerations
- 8″ × 10″ (1/3)
- Detail cassette

### Positioning
- Pronate hand, which puts thumb in oblique position

### Central Ray
- Perpendicular to metacarpophalangeal joint

### Radiograph Evaluation Criteria
- Soft tissue structures and trapezium included
- Cortex and trabeculae visualized and sharp
- Proximal and distal phalanges, metacarpal demonstrated
- Interphalangeal joint, metacarpophalangeal joint, and carpometacarpal joint demonstrated

---

NOTES

T

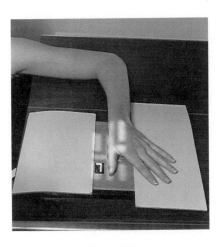

## OBLIQUE THUMB

| Patient Size | kVp | mAs |
|---|---|---|
| | | |
| | | |
| | | |
| | | |
| | | |
| | | |
| | | |
| | | |
| | | |

T

## ▸ THUMB: LATERAL (1ST DIGIT)

### Technical Considerations
- 8″ × 10″ (1/3)
- Detail cassette

### Positioning
- Thumb in true lateral position

### Central Ray
- Perpendicular to metacarpophalangeal joint

### Radiograph Evaluation Criteria
- Soft tissue structures and trapezium included
- Cortex and trabeculae visualized and sharp
- Proximal and distal phalanges, metacarpal demonstrated
- Interphalangeal joint, metacarpophalangeal joint, and carpometacarpal joint demonstrated

---

NOTES

T

| LATERAL THUMB | | |
| --- | --- | --- |
| Patient Size | kVp | mAs |
| | | |
| | | |
| | | |
| | | |
| | | |
| | | |
| | | |
| | | |

T

## ► TOES: AP

### Technical Considerations
- 8″ × 10″ (1/3)
- Detail cassette

### Positioning
- Plantar surface of foot on cassette

### Central Ray
- Perpendicular to metatarsophalangeal joint

### Radiograph Evaluation Criteria
- Soft tissue structures and half of metatarsal included
- Cortex and trabeculae visualized
- Phalanges, interphalangeal joints, and metatarsophalangeal joint demonstrated

---

NOTES

T

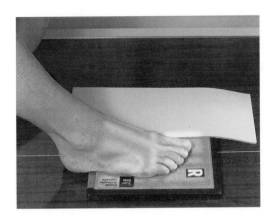

## AP TOES

| Patient Size | kVp | mAs |
|---|---|---|
| | | |
| | | |
| | | |
| | | |
| | | |
| | | |
| | | |
| | | |
| | | |

## ► TOES: MEDIAL OBLIQUE

### Technical Considerations
- 8″ × 10″ (1/3)
- Detail cassette

### Positioning
- Rotate foot 30°

### Central Ray
- Perpendicular to metatarsophalangeal joint

### Radiograph Evaluation Criteria
- Soft tissue structures and half of metatarsal included
- Cortex and trabeculae visualized
- Phalanges, interphalangeal joints, and metatarsophalangeal joint demonstrated

---

NOTES

T

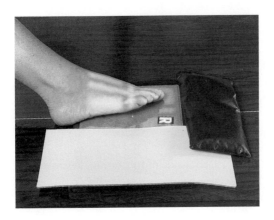

## MEDIAL OBLIQUE TOES

| Patient Size | kVp | mAs |
|---|---|---|
| | | |
| | | |
| | | |
| | | |
| | | |
| | | |
| | | |
| | | |
| | | |
| | | |

T

## ▶ TOES: LATERAL

### Technical Considerations
- 8″ × 10″ (1/3)
- Detail cassette

### Positioning
- Toe in true lateral
- Medial or lateral side of foot down, depending on which toe is affected
- Move unaffected toes away

### Central Ray
- Perpendicular to interphalangeal or proximal interphalangeal joint

### Radiograph Evaluation Criteria
- Soft tissue structures and distal metatarsal included
- Cortex and trabeculae visualized
- Phalanges, interphalangeal joints, and metatarsophalangeal joint demonstrated

---

NOTES

T

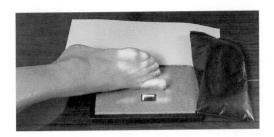

## LATERAL TOE (1ST DIGIT)

| Patient Size | kVp | mAs |
|---|---|---|
| | | |
| | | |
| | | |
| | | |
| | | |
| | | |
| | | |
| | | |
| | | |
| | | |
| | | |

T

## ► WRIST: PA

### Technical Considerations
- 8″ × 10″ (1/2) or 10″ × 12″ (1/3)
- Detail cassette

### Positioning
- Fingers flexed so wrist is flat
- Elbow flexed 90°

### Central Ray
- Perpendicular to midcarpal area

### Radiograph Evaluation Criteria
- Soft tissue structures, metacarpals, and 2″ distal radius and ulna included
- Cortex and trabeculae visualized
- Scaphoid, lunate, capitate, and hamate demonstrated

---

NOTES

W

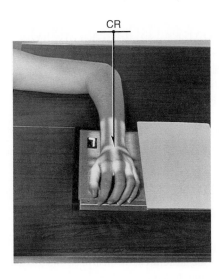

| PA WRIST | | |
|---|---|---|
| Patient Size | kVp | mAs |
| | | |
| | | |
| | | |
| | | |
| | | |
| | | |
| | | |
| | | |

W

# ► WRIST: PA OBLIQUE (SEMIPRONATION)

## Technical Considerations
- 8″ × 10″ (1/2) or 10″ × 12″ (1/3)
- Detail cassette

## Positioning
- Rotate wrist 45° laterally from pronated position
- Elbow flexed 90°

## Central Ray
- Perpendicular to midcarpal area

## Radiograph Evaluation Criteria
- Soft tissue structures, metacarpals, and 2″ distal radius and ulna included
- Cortex and trabeculae visualized
- Trapezium, trapezoid, lunate, scaphoid, and 1st carpometacarpal joint demonstrated

---

NOTES

W

## PA OBLIQUE WRIST

| Patient Size | kVp | mAs |
| --- | --- | --- |
| | | |
| | | |
| | | |
| | | |
| | | |
| | | |
| | | |

W

## ▶ WRIST: AP OBLIQUE (SEMISUPINATION)

### Technical Considerations
- 8″ × 10″ (1/2)  or 10″ × 12″ (1/3)
- Detail cassette

### Positioning
- Rotate wrist 45° medially from supinated position
- Elbow flexed 90°

### Central Ray
- Perpendicular to midcarpal area

### Radiograph Evaluation Criteria
- Soft tissue structures, metacarpals, and 2″ distal radius and ulna included
- Cortex and trabeculae visualized
- Pisiform separated from triquetrum
- Triquetrum and hamate demonstrated

---

NOTES

W

CR

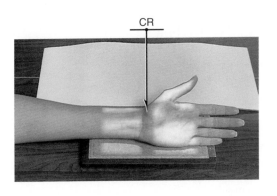

## AP OBLIQUE WRIST

| Patient Size | kVp | mAs |
|---|---|---|
| | | |
| | | |
| | | |
| | | |
| | | |
| | | |
| | | |
| | | |
| | | |
| | | |

W

## ▶ WRIST: LATERAL

### Technical Considerations
- 8″ × 10″ (1/2) or 10″ × 12″ (1/3)
- Detail cassette

### Positioning
- Wrist in true lateral with 5th finger resting on cassette
- Elbow flexed 90°

### Central Ray
- Perpendicular to midcarpal area

### Radiograph Evaluation Criteria
- Soft tissue structures, metacarpals, and 2″ distal radius and ulna included
- Cortex and trabeculae visualized
- Head of ulna superimposed over distal radius
- Trapezium, lunate, and pisiform demonstrated

---

NOTES

W

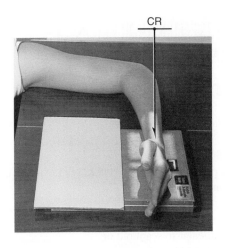

| LATERAL WRIST | | |
|---|---|---|
| Patient Size | kVp | mAs |
| | | |
| | | |
| | | |
| | | |
| | | |
| | | |
| | | |
| | | |
| | | |

W

# ► WRIST: ULNAR FLEXION (RADIAL DEVIATION)

## Technical Considerations
- 8″ × 10″ (1/2)
- Detail cassette

## Positioning
- Hand pronated and flexed laterally in extreme ulnar flexion

## Central Ray
- Perpendicular to scaphoid **or**
- 15–20° toward the forearm

## Radiograph Evaluation Criteria
- Soft tissue structures, proximal metacarpals, and 1″ distal radius and ulna included
- Cortex and trabeculae visualized
- Scaphoid, lunate, trapezium, and trapezoid demonstrated

---

NOTES

W

CR

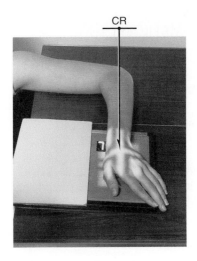

| ULNAR FLEXION WRIST | | |
|---|---|---|
| Patient Size | kVp | mAs |
| | | |
| | | |
| | | |
| | | |
| | | |
| | | |
| | | |
| | | |

W

## ▶ ZYGOMATIC ARCHES: SUBMENTOVERTICAL

### Technical Considerations
- 8″ × 10″ or 9″ × 9″ cassette
- Grid or non-grid

### Positioning
- Head and neck hyperextended
- Infraorbitomeatal line parallel or nearly parallel with plane of film
- Vertex resting on grid device

### Central Ray
- Perpendicular to infraorbitomeatal line to point midway between gonia at level of zygomatic arches

### Radiograph Evaluation Criteria
- Both zygomatic arches included
- Zygomatic arches adequately penetrated
- Bilateral symmetrical zygomatic arches demonstrated

---

NOTES

## SUBMENTOVERTICAL ZYGOMATIC ARCHES

| Patient Size | kVp | mAs |
|---|---|---|
| | | |
| | | |
| | | |
| | | |
| | | |
| | | |
| | | |
| | | |
| | | |

## ► ZYGOMATIC ARCHES: TANGENTIAL

### Technical Considerations
- 8″ × 10″ or 9″ × 9″ cassette
- Grid or non-grid

### Positioning
- Head and neck hyperextended
- Infraorbitomeatal line parallel or nearly parallel with plane of film
- Vertex resting on grid device
- Rotate head 15° toward side of interest

### Central Ray
- Perpendicular to infraorbitomeatal line through zygomatic arch of interest

### Radiograph Evaluation Criteria
- Zygomatic arch adequately penetrated
- Zygomatic arch demonstrated free of superimposition by adjacent structures
- Zygomatic arch nearest the film demonstrated

---

NOTES

Z

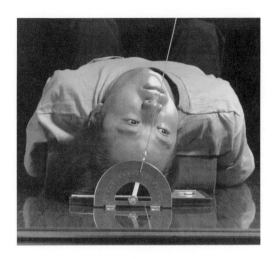

| TANGENTIAL ZYGOMATIC ARCHES | | |
| --- | --- | --- |
| Patient Size | kVp | mAs |
| | | |
| | | |
| | | |
| | | |
| | | |
| | | |
| | | |

Z

# APPENDICES

........................................................................................

APPENDIX A

# CAST CONVERSIONS

| | |
|---|---|
| Small/medium dry plaster | Increase 5–7 kVp |
| Large/wet plaster | Increases 8–10 kVp or double mAs |
| Wet fiberglass | Increase 0–4 kVp |
| Dry fiberglass | Usually no change |

APPENDIX B

# COMMON DIAGNOSIS-RELATED ABBREVIATIONS

| | |
|---|---|
| AK | above knee |
| ALL | acute lymphocytic leukemia |
| ALS | amyotrophic lateral sclerosis |
| AMI | acute myocardial infarction |
| AODM | adult onset diabetes mellitus |
| ARDS | adult respiratory distress syndrome |
| ADS | atrial septal defect |
| ASCVD | arteriosclerotic cardiovascular disease |
| ASD | atrial septal defect |
| ASHD | arteriosclerotic heart disease |
| | |
| BK | below knee |
| BPH | benign prostatic hypertrophy |
| | |
| CA | cancer |
| CAD | coronary artery disease |
| CF | cystic fibrosis |
| CHD | coronary heart disease |
| CHF | congestive heart failure |

| | |
|---|---|
| CLL | chronic lymphocytic leukemia |
| CML | chronic myelocytic leukemia |
| CP | cerebral palsy |
| COPD | chronic obstructive pulmonary disease |
| CRF | chronic renal failure |
| CVA | cerebral vascular accident |
| D & C | dilation and curettage |
| DJD | degenerative joint disease |
| DKA | diabetic ketoacidosis |
| DM | diabetes mellitus |
| DOE | dyspnea on exertion |
| FUO | fever of unknown origin |
| FWB | full weight-bearing |
| Fx | fracture |
| HNP | herniated nucleus pulposus |
| HSV | herpes simplex virus |
| HT, HTN | hypertension |
| HVD | hypertensive vascular disease |
| IC | irritable colon |
| LE | lupus erythematosus; lower extremity |
| LVH | left ventricular hypertrophy |
| MD | muscular dystrophy |
| MI | myocardial infarction |
| MS | multiple sclerosis; mitral stenosis |
| NKA | no known allergies |
| N & V | nausea and vomiting |
| NWB | non–weight-bearing |

| | |
|---|---|
| PE | pulmonary embolism |
| PID | pelvic inflammatory disease |
| PVC | premature ventricular contractions |
| | |
| RA | rheumatoid arthritis |
| RDS | respiratory distress syndrome |
| RHD | rheumatic heart disease |
| R/O | rule out |
| | |
| SGA | small for gestational age |
| SIDS | sudden infant death syndrome |
| SLE | systemic lupus erythematosus |
| SOB | shortness of breath |
| S/P | status post |
| STD | sexually transmitted disease |
| | |
| TB | tuberculosis |
| TIA | transient ischemic attack |
| TUR | transurethral resection |
| TURP | transurethral prostatectomy |
| | |
| UE | upper extremity |
| URI | upper respiratory infection |
| UTI | urinary tract infection |
| | |
| VD | venereal disease |
| | |
| WB | weight-bearing |

APPENDIX C

# GRID CONVERSION FACTORS

Converting from non-grid to grid technique:

| | |
|---|---|
| 5:1 grid ratio | $2 \times mAs$ |
| 6:1 grid ratio | $3 \times mAs$ |
| 8:1 grid ratio | $4 \times mAs$ |
| 12:1 grid ratio | $5 \times mAs$ |
| 16:1 grid ratio | $6 \times mAs$ |

APPENDIX

# PATHOLOGICAL CONDITIONS

---

### SKELETAL PATHOLOGICAL CONDITIONS

| Additive *(hard to penetrate)* | Destructive *(easy to penetrate)* |
| --- | --- |
| Acromegaly | Active osteomyelitis |
| Callus | Atrophy |
| Exostosis | Carcinoma |
| Hydrocephalus | Degenerative arthritis |
| Osteoma | Ewing tumor |
| Osteopetrosis | Gout |
| Paget's disease | Hodgkin's disease |
| Sclerosis | Neuroblastoma |
| | Osteoporosis |

---

### RESPIRATORY PATHOLOGICAL CONDITIONS

| Additive *(hard to penetrate)* | Destructive *(easy to penetrate)* |
| --- | --- |
| Atelectasis | Emphysema |
| Bronchiectasis | Pneumothorax |
| Empyema | |
| Malignancy | |
| Pleural effusion | |
| Pneumoconiosis | |
| Pneumonia | |
| Pulmonary edema | |

APPENDIX E

# SKULL LANDMARKS AND LINES

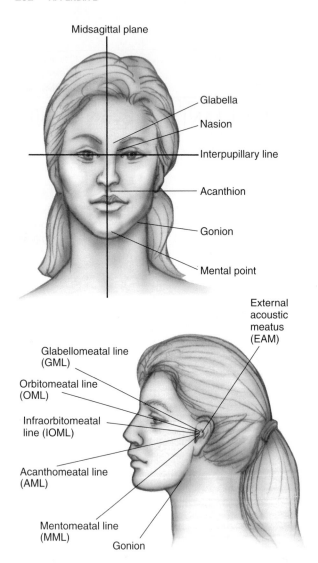

Midsagittal plane

Glabella

Nasion

Interpupillary line

Acanthion

Gonion

Mental point

External acoustic meatus (EAM)

Glabellomeatal line (GML)

Orbitomeatal line (OML)

Infraorbitomeatal line (IOML)

Acanthomeatal line (AML)

Mentomeatal line (MML)

Gonion

# INDEX